THE BIBLE STORY

VOLUME VIII

—•—

PRINCE OF PRINCES

(From His Early Ministry to His Last Parables)

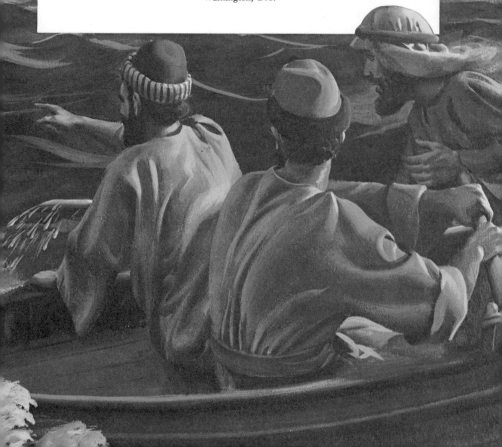

The

BIBLE STORY

More Than Four Hundred Stories in Ten Volumes
Covering the Entire Bible From Genesis to Revelation

VOLUME EIGHT
Prince of Princes

BY ARTHUR S. MAXWELL

Author of *Uncle Arthur's Bedtime Stories, The Children's Hour With Uncle Arthur, The Secret of the Cave,* etc.

•

REVIEW AND HERALD PUBLISHING ASSOCIATION
Washington, D.C.

CONTENTS

Part I—Stories of the Prince of Healers

MATTHEW 9:18-32; 12:10-13; 14:22-15:28; 20:30-34; MARK 1:40-45; 5:21-7:37; 7:31-37; 10:46-52; LUKE 7:18-35; 9:12-17; 17:11-19; 18:35-19:9; JOHN 5:1-19; 6:1-14

Part II—Stories of the Prince of Teachers

MATTHEW 5:1-7:27; 17:1-18:35; 20:20-28; MARK 7:1-23; 10:32-40; LUKE 6:1-49; 9:28-42; 10:38-14:6

5

— PAINTING BY RUSSELL HARLAN   © 1956, BY REVIEW AND HERALD

he pure, trusting innocence of children found
inship with the gentleness and tenderness of
esus. Putting His hands upon them in blessing
e said, "Of such is the kingdom of heaven."

Part III—Stories of the Prince of Storytellers

MATTHEW 13:1-50; 18:23-35; 21:28-22:14; MARK 12:1-44; LUKE 8:4-15; 10:25-37; 14:16-15:32; 18:9-14; 20:9-19

Part IV—Stories of the Prince of Prophets

MATTHEW 24:1-25:46; MARK 13:1-37; LUKE 17:21-37; 19:12-27; 21:1-36; JOHN 13:36-14:3

PART I

Stories of the Prince of Healers

(MATTHEW 9:18-32; 12:10-13; 14:22-15:28; 20:30-34; MARK
1:40-45; 5:21-7:37; 7:31-37; 10:46-52; LUKE 7:18-35; 9:12-17;
17:11-19; 18:35-19:9; JOHN 5:1-19; 6:1-14)

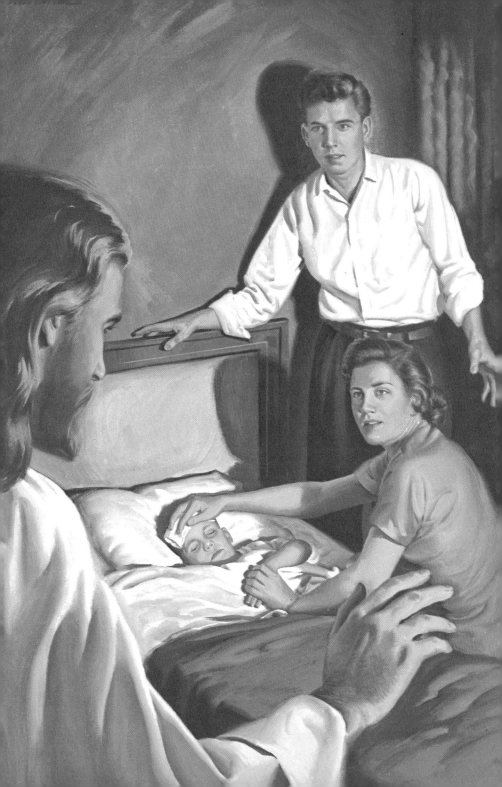

STORY 1

Withered Hand Made Whole

THINGS had gone hard for the poor old man ever since he first felt the pain in his hand. He could remember the day it began. Then, as weeks and months had passed, it had got worse and worse until his finger joints were all stiff and he couldn't bend his wrist. Later his hand had gradually shriveled up until he couldn't use it at all.

That meant he couldn't work. So he had lost his job and his income and had even had to beg for food.

He had asked the doctors to help him, but they didn't know how to treat a withered hand. They had just told him he would have to put up with it for the rest of his life. It was all very sad and discouraging.

Then one Sabbath he went into the synagogue in Capernaum. As he took his seat he hid his poor hand under his robe, where no one could see it. He didn't like people staring at it out of curiosity. Then he prayed the prayer he had prayed so many times before, "Dear God, help me!"

9

PAINTING BY RUSSELL HARLAN   © 1956, BY REVIEW AND HERALD

esus was the prince of healers. He entered
e homes of both poor and rich, and every-
here He went He left gladness and rejoicing
 a result of His wonderful healing touch.

Suddenly he became aware that, for some reason or other, he had become the center of interest in the synagogue. Everybody was staring at him. He was frightened, wondering what he could have done. Surely all these people were not just looking to see his withered hand!

No, it couldn't be that, for he noticed that their heads kept turning from him to another Man, then back to him. The other Man was the one they called the Carpenter of Nazareth.

Now the Carpenter Himself was looking at him, and he felt the warmth of friendship and sympathy in His eyes.

"Arise; stand forth in the midst," said the Carpenter in a kindly voice.

"What, me?"

"Yes, you."

Wondering what it could all mean, the poor old man, still keeping his withered hand covered, did as he was told. Now everybody *was* looking at him.

"Stretch forth your hand," said the gentle Carpenter.

"My poor hand?"

"Yes, your poor hand."

Slowly he pulled it out from beneath his robe. Suddenly his eyes opened wide in astonishment. Then they filled with tears. For his hand wasn't shriveled any more. It was just like his other hand! He could move his fingers! He could bend his wrist! He could touch his face! It was too good to be true; but it *was* true.

"Thank You, thank You, Master!" I can hear him saying.

10

WITHERED HAND MADE WHOLE

But the other voices were not thankful.

"He shouldn't have done it!" grumbled one. "The idea of doing such a thing on the holy Sabbath!" said another. "It's shocking," shouted a third; "the man's a lawbreaker and should be arrested."

"Is it lawful to do good on the Sabbath days, or to do evil?" Jesus asked them. "To save life, or to kill?"

No one answered Him.

As for the old man, he didn't understand what they were all arguing about. He just kept looking at his hand and moving it to and fro. He couldn't get over it. It was the best thing that had ever happened to him on the Sabbath. In church, too.

His hand had been healed! Now he could work again! Thank God! O wonderful, wonderful Jesus!

STORY   2

Sick Woman Healed

ONE DAY as Jesus was teaching on the beach by the Sea of Galilee He saw a man pushing his way through the crowd. The man seemed to be in a great hurry and very much upset about something.

"Pardon me, please let me pass," he was saying. "I must get through to Jesus at once. Make way! *Please* make way! It's very urgent."

It was Jairus, a ruler of the synagogue, and he was troubled about his little girl.

Falling to his knees before Jesus he told Him what was the matter and earnestly begged for help.

"My little daughter is at the point of death," he cried. "Please come and lay Your hands on her, so that she may be made well and live."

Jesus' heart was touched. He knew what it must have meant for a ruler of the synagogue to kneel and ask Him for help. How great must be this man's love for his little girl!

SICK WOMAN HEALED

"I'll go with you," said Jesus, and Jairus was delighted. But as the two started on their way the crowd surged around them. It was hard to make any progress. So many people wanted to get close to Jesus, to look at Him, to touch Him.

They had not gone very far when suddenly Jesus stood still.

"Who touched my clothes?" He asked.

It was a strange question, with so many hundreds of people pushing and shoving about Him.

The disciples were surprised. "How can You ask who touched You when there are so many people around You?" they said.

But Jesus knew somebody had touched Him. Somebody in great need. Somebody whose faith had already drawn healing power from Him.

He looked around. Who of all these many, many people could it be?

Then He saw her. There was no mistaking who it was. Tears of joy and thankfulness were running down her cheeks.

Jesus understood. He smiled at her while she "fell down before Him, and told Him all the truth."

She had been sick twelve years, she said. All this long time she had gone from one doctor to another without getting any help. She had spent all her money on doctors' bills, and still the bleeding from which she suffered continued. Then she had said to herself, "If I may but touch His garment, I shall be whole." So she had touched Him. It was only a light touch, on "the hem of His garment." She hadn't meant to trouble Him, for she knew He was so busy looking after all the other needy people. And then, all of a sudden, she had felt better. Just like that. Her wound had healed. The bleeding had stopped. She knew it for sure. And she was so thankful. So very, very thankful.

Jesus was thankful too; thankful that somebody had trusted Him so much. I like to think that He gently patted the poor woman's head as she knelt there before Him. "Daughter," He said to her, "your faith has made you well; go in peace, and be healed of your disease."

The woman disappeared in the crowd, but not from history. Somebody saw and heard what happened and wrote it down so that you and I today may know that we may reach out and touch Him by faith in every time of need.

STORY 3

Dead Girl Lives Again

≋≋≋≋≋≋≋≋≋≋≋≋≋≋≋≋≋≋≋≋≋≋≋

W HILE all this was going on Jairus was standing by, impatient to get back to his dying daughter. Perhaps he tugged at Jesus' sleeve, urging Him to make haste.

"Please!" he may have said, "Do come soon! She may die any minute."

And then she was dead.

A messenger pressed through the crowd bringing Jairus the sad news.

"Your daughter is dead," he said. "Why trouble the Master any more?"

People around said, "Oh!" and began to say how sorry they were. Poor Jairus just stood there, too sad to speak. Tears rolled down his cheeks. He had loved his little girl so much!

Jesus looked at him in great pity. "Don't worry," He said, "only believe."

Then He began to walk toward Jairus' house again.

There wasn't much use of His going there now, Jairus thought. If only that woman hadn't stopped Him! Then He might have been in time. And what did Jesus mean by saying, "Don't worry; only believe"? The child was dead. What could He do now? What could anybody do save bury the poor little dear?

The crowd tried to follow Jesus, but He asked them kindly but firmly to go away. It wouldn't be proper for so many to visit a home so full of sadness. Peter, James, and John could go with Him, but no one else. He was quite strict about it, and the people obeyed Him.

As the little group drew near to Jairus' house they saw a strange sight. Many of the neighbors were trying to push their way through the front door, but couldn't get in. The place was crowded with people. Some were friends of the family; some were just sight-seers.

From inside came sounds of weeping and wailing. It was the custom in those days to employ "mourners" who made sorrowful noises at funerals, and these were doing their part well. They "wept and wailed greatly," the Bible says.

As Jesus arrived the people gave way and let Him in. Jairus and the three disciples followed.

"Why make all this noise?" asked Jesus. "The little girl is not dead. She's just sleeping."

The mourners stopped their make-believe wailing and started to laugh. "She's dead all right," one of them said. "Go and see for yourself."

"Please leave," said Jesus. And He said it so sternly that

16

they did what He said. In a little while all of them had shuffled out the door, and the house was quiet again. Then Jesus led the sorrowing father and mother, with Peter, James, and John, into the room where the little girl was lying so white and still upon her bed.

As Mother and Father sobbed in their grief Jesus looked down at the child in great tenderness. Then He smiled at her and said, "Little girl, I say to you, Arise."

It was just as though He had said, "It's time to get up, darling," and she woke up, right then and there. Then she jumped out of bed just as if she had never been sick. And I wouldn't be surprised if the first thing she said was, "Mummy, what are you crying for?"

But the tears were all over now. Mother hugged her close. She didn't know whether to laugh or cry, she was so happy. So was Father. So were Peter, James, and John. And so, I believe, was Jesus. He loved to make people happy. He would have liked to make every home in all the world as happy as this one was right now.

And I like to think that before He said good-by the little girl came up to Him and said, very sweetly and simply, out of her heart, "Thank You, kind Teacher. I love You."

STORY 4

Needy Foreigner Helped

AFTER teaching and healing for several months in Galilee, Jesus traveled to the Mediterranean coast, then northward into Tyre and Sidon.

Here He was on foreign soil, outside the boundaries of Israel. It was just as foreign as Mexico is to the United States, or as France is to England, or as China is to Australia. The disciples must have wondered why He had come here. His message was only for the Jews, they thought. Surely He would never heal any of these Gentiles, these foreigners.

Then they got a surprise.

One day a woman followed the little group that had come with Jesus on this trip.

Somehow, even this far north, she must have heard about Him and His power to heal, for she cried to Him, "Have mercy on me, O Lord, Thou son of David; my daughter is grievously vexed with a devil."

At first Jesus took no notice. No doubt this was because

He wanted to see what would happen next and what His disciples would say.

Meanwhile the woman continued to call to Him, "Have mercy on me, O Lord, Thou son of David. Have mercy! Have mercy!"

The disciples became annoyed. "Send her away," they urged Him. "She is crying after us."

They saw she was a foreigner. How could such a person expect any help from their Messiah? She had better be sent about her business.

Now Jesus stood still and the woman drew near. Falling at His feet she cried, "Lord, help me!"

Such a cry, no matter from whom it comes, whether from Jew or Gentile, American or Englishman, Frenchman or German, Australian or African, ever finds a response in the heart of Jesus. But this time there was a lesson for the disciples to learn. So, speaking as they might have done, He said, "It is not fair to take the children's bread and throw it to the dogs."

NEEDY FOREIGNER HELPED

The woman answered, humbly and earnestly, "Yes, Lord, yet even the dogs eat the crumbs that fall from their master's table."

It was a wonderful answer from someone who was not an Israelite. It showed that she believed Jesus could help anyone, anywhere.

"O woman," Jesus said to her, "great is your faith! Be it done for you as you desire."

That very moment her daughter was healed.

The disciples were astonished. Their beloved Master had answered the prayer of a foreigner! Clearly there was nothing narrow or national about Him. Could it be that He had come to bless not only "the lost sheep of the house of Israel" but all the lost sheep of all the nations in all the wide, wide world? It was only an idea, a beautiful idea, but it began to grow and grow in their minds as the days and the years passed by.

STORY 5

Lonely Prisoner Cheered

WHILE Jesus was busy helping all the needy people and teaching them about His kingdom of love, He never forgot his poor cousin John whom Herod had put in prison. His heart of love went out in pity to this mighty preacher of righteousness who was now locked up where he could never preach again.

One day two men brought Jesus a message from John, and it showed how discouraged the poor prisoner had become. "Art thou He that should come?" he asked, "or look we for another?"

How different was this from what he had said about Jesus a little while before: "Behold the Lamb of God, which taketh away the sin of the world."

It was clear that he had begun to doubt whether Jesus was really the Messiah after all. Perhaps he was wondering why He had not come long since to set him free. But Jesus did not rebuke him. He understood how John must be feeling,

22

and how hard it is to be brave and hopeful in a dungeon.

So, for John's special benefit, and to cheer his fainting heart, Jesus revealed His power as He had never done before. Quickly, "in that same hour," He went from one to another of the sick people about Him, healing them of their sicknesses. He cast out evil spirits, opened the eyes of the blind, and gave hearing to the deaf. He even raised the dead.

Never were so many people blessed in so short a time. It was a mighty revelation of the power of God.

When the last sick person near Him had been healed Jesus turned to the two men who had come from John—and who had been gazing open-mouthed at all these miracles— and told them to go and tell John all that they had seen and heard, "how that the blind see, the lame walk, the lepers are cleansed, the deaf hear, the dead are raised, to the poor the gospel is preached. And blessed is he, whosoever shall not be offended in Me."

It was as if Jesus had said to John, "Cheer up! Our cause is not lost. You may be beheaded; I may be crucified; but love will win in the end."

After John's messengers had left, their hearts full of new courage, Jesus went on to talk about His cousin to the people who remained.

"What did you go into the wilderness to see?" He asked them. "A reed shaken in the wind?"

No wind-blown reed was John, but a rock of strength.

"Well, did you go out to see a man in soft raiment, living like men in the courts of kings?"

No courtier was John, but a fearless preacher of God's Word.

"Well, did you go out to see a prophet?"

Yes. That is what he was. "And much more than a prophet." And why? Because he fulfilled prophecy. He was the one of whom Malachi had spoken when he said, "Behold, I will send my messenger, and he shall prepare the way before me." John prepared the way for Jesus. He was the forerunner of the Messiah.

The people who listened were happy that Jesus spoke so well of John and his work, for most of them had been baptized by him and still held him in high regard. Some of them no doubt carried Jesus' words to John to bring new courage to the lonely prisoner.

How glad he must have been to learn that he was not mistaken about Jesus and that He was indeed "the Lamb of God" after all!

STORY 6

Dumb Man Speaks

WHEN Jesus returned to Galilee from Tyre and Sidon a deaf-and-dumb man was brought to Him. Here was a new problem. Nobody in those days knew how to help anybody like this. There were no hearing aids for the deaf or special clinics for the dumb. The poor folks who were troubled like this lived in total silence, with no idea what a baby's cry might be, or the laughter of a child, or a bar of music. Nor could they ever hope to tell their children that they loved them, or talk with their friends, or say their prayers out loud.

Even in the presence of Jesus this poor man couldn't say, "Lord, help me!" nor could he hear a word that Jesus said.

But Jesus understood. Though not a word was spoken, Jesus heard the cry in the poor man's heart. Leading him away from the crowd, He found a place where they could be alone. Then He put His fingers in the man's ears, and touched his tongue. Looking heavenward, He cried, "Be opened!"

25

and immediately the man was able to both hear and speak.

What a glorious moment that must have been for him! His whole world was changed. The years of silence were over. He could hear the birds sing and the children laugh and the voices of his neighbors as they rejoiced in his healing. And the first words he ever heard were the words of Jesus bidding him be well.

How wonderful it must have been for him to be able to talk like other people! For a while, I imagine, he couldn't stop talking. So much that he had wanted to say had been bottled up inside him for years. Now it came pouring out in an endless stream.

And what do you suppose he said first? Wouldn't you like to know? So would I. Somehow I think it must have been, "Jesus, O Jesus, thank You! Thank You for opening my ears and loosening my tongue. For this I will love You always."

As for the people, they were "beyond measure astonished, saying, He hath done all things well."

He surely had.

PAINTING BY PAUL REMMEY, ARTIST

STORY 7

Blind Man Sees

BARTIMAEUS was sitting by the roadside near the city of Jericho, begging for money from passers-by.

How many years he had sat in this same place day after day, he couldn't remember. It was a long, long time. Travelers between Jericho and Jerusalem had come to expect to see him here. When still quite a long way off they could hear his plaintive plea, "Help the blind! Please help the blind!"

He didn't know the meaning of the word "sight," for he had been blind from birth. Never once had he seen a flower, or a tree, or a house, or his mother's face.

People had told him about these things. He had tried to imagine what sunshine must be like, but it was very difficult. He lived in a world of darkness, and there was no way out.

His senses of touch and hearing were very keen, and he could find his way about very well, but he could never see anything. Nothing.

Oh, how he longed to be able to see! It had been his dearest wish since his childhood. As a little boy he had hoped that maybe when he grew up he might be able to see like other people, but now that he was old he knew there was no hope. None.

Well, not exactly. Once, some time ago, hope had come to his heart again. It was when a passer-by had told him about a wonderful Teacher who had appeared in Galilee, who was healing people of the worst diseases. He had even healed lepers, and made the dumb to speak and the deaf to hear. Yes, He had even opened the eyes of the blind.

"But don't get excited about it," the stranger had said. "He's away up in Galilee and most likely will never come to Jericho."

"Oh!" thought poor Bartimaeus, "if only He would come this way, just once!"

He thought about this many times. Now and then he would ask people whether they knew anything about the great Teacher who opened the eyes of the blind. Some had heard of Him and some hadn't. But nobody expected Him to come to Jericho.

"And even if He did," someone said, "He probably wouldn't see you anyway. There are always hundreds of people around Him, all wanting something."

"But," thought Bartimaeus, as hope faded again, "if He ever does come, I'll be on the roadside waiting for Him."

Then one day it happened.

It had been a warm, sunny, sultry afternoon, like so many others in this part of the Jordan valley. Very few people were traveling, and very little money had been placed in his outstretched hand. It seemed as though everybody must be staying in the city for some reason or other, and he didn't know why. Now and then he could hear shouting in the distance, but he couldn't guess what it was all about.

Then the sound grew louder, and he recognized it as that of a great crowd moving. It was coming nearer and nearer along the Jericho road. He guessed there must be hundreds of people in the noisy throng, and he wondered why.

"What is it?" he asked a passer-by. "What's the matter?"

BLIND MAN SEES

"Jesus of Nazareth is passing by," said the stranger.

"Not Jesus of Nazareth!" cried Bartimaeus. Then to himself, "So He has come at last! Oh, I must not miss Him now!"

As the sound of the scuffling feet and the many voices became louder and louder he guessed the great Teacher must be coming very near. And soon He would be gone. It must be now or never.

Suddenly he shouted at the top of his voice, "Jesus, Thou Son of David, have mercy on me!"

All the longing of his soul was in that cry. All that he had hoped for through all his poor, sad life.

Nothing happened. Only more and more people went hurrying by. So he cried again as loud as he could, "Jesus! Jesus! Thou Son of David, have mercy on me!"

He was desperate. He *must* let Jesus know he was here. But there was so much noise. So many people. "Jesus!" he cried again, and louder still.

"Be quiet!" snapped somebody. "Don't shout so! The Master's bothered enough anyway."

But Bartimaeus took no notice. This was his one great chance. It might never come again. So "he cried the more a great deal, Thou son of David, have mercy on me."

Then it seemed to him as though the crowd stopped moving. A moment later, and very close by, he heard a voice full of kindness and love saying, "Bring him to Me."

Next he heard another voice saying, "Come on, Bartimaeus. Take heart. The Master is calling you."

Bartimaeus didn't need anyone to show him the way. The voice of Jesus drew him like a magnet.

"What do you want Me to do for you?" asked Jesus.

So Jesus had heard him! Above all the noise of the crowd the cry of one poor blind man had reached His ears!

"Lord!" cried Bartimaeus, "that I might receive my sight!"

"Go," said Jesus; "your faith has made you whole."

And it had; for "immediately he received his sight." His eyes opened, and the very first thing he saw was the face of Jesus smiling upon him in tender sympathy.

No wonder the Bible says that he "followed Jesus in the way." I am sure he did. All the way, to the end of life's journey.

STORY 8

Old Cripple Walks

S O EAGER was Jesus to help the poor and needy that sometimes He sought them out in their strange hiding places.

One Sabbath afternoon when He was on a brief visit to Jerusalem He went down to the pool of Bethesda to see the scores of sick folks who gathered there under its five arches.

They were a sad sight. Some were lame; some were blind; some were paralyzed. Each one believed that if only he could get into the pool at the right time he would be healed. Day in and day out, week in and week out, each one kept hoping that he would be the next one to be healed.

As Jesus looked upon all these poor sufferers His heart of love was deeply touched. He spoke to one of them and learned that he had been a cripple for thirty-eight years.

Thirty-eight years! And all this long, long time he had been hoping he might get better! How very, very sad!

"Do you want to be healed?" asked Jesus.

OLD CRIPPLE WALKS

Did he! But he had lost hope. There was nobody to help him into the pool. It took him so long to wriggle over to the edge that somebody always got there before he did.

But Jesus knew how to bring new hope to the hopeless.

Tenderly but firmly He said to the poor cripple, "Rise, take up your bed and walk."

Walk! The poor man scarcely knew what the word meant. He hadn't walked for so many, many years. He was so weak, so stiff, so——but no, he wasn't. Not any more. Something had happened inside him. He struggled to get up. There was no pain. He found he could bend his knees. He could stand! True, he was a bit shaky, but getting steadier all the time. It was wonderful! Then he stooped to pick up his bed, or pallet, just as Jesus had told him to, and it didn't hurt to bend. He was healed! He was well! He could walk and run and jump again—after thirty-eight years! Wonder of wonders! It was too good to be true.

So excited was he at finding himself well that he never noticed who it was who had healed him. When he looked around to thank Him, Jesus had gone. So he walked out through one of the five arches— right into trouble.

A group of people outside asked him what he meant by carrying his bed on the Sabbath.

Sabbath? He had quite forgotten that it was the Sabbath, so happy was he at having been healed.

"The man who healed me said, 'Take up your bed and walk,'" he said innocently.

"Who told you that?" they asked.

"The man who healed me."

"And who was it?" they insisted.

"I don't know."

And he didn't. But a little while later, when he went to the Temple to thank God for being healed, he met Jesus again. Jesus now told him not to sin any more lest something worse should happen to him.

Then he recognized Jesus as the One who had healed him.

"That's the Man!" he told those who had asked him why he was carrying his bed on the Sabbath. But they had already guessed that it was Jesus.

Foolishly they were all upset because Jesus had "broken" the Sabbath—as they thought—instead of rejoicing that one of God's suffering children had found health and happiness on His sacred day. They must learn that "the Sabbath was made for man, and not man for the Sabbath."

STORY 9

Lepers Cleansed

D ID YOU ever stop to think that though Jesus was always mixing with sick people, He never got sick Himself? Tired, yes, but not sick. We never read of His having mumps or measles or chickenpox or anything like that.

He was like a fountain of life, pouring forth health, strength, and happiness to others. "I am come that they might have life," He said once; and that is what He was giving away all day long and every day.

That is why people flocked to Him by hundreds and thousands. They all wanted to be well and strong, and here was Someone who knew the secret. Better than any doctor, He was able to cure the worst diseases, and quickly, too. No sickness seemed too hard for Him. Not even leprosy.

In those days nothing frightened people more than the thought of catching this dread disease. Those who caught it had to leave their homes and villages and live with other lepers wherever they could find shelter. And there they gradually got worse and worse till they died.

One day a leper, seeing Jesus in the distance, forgot all the rules about staying away from other people, and came running toward Him.

"Go away! Go away!" I can hear the bystanders crying as they moved back, scared to death. "Get out of here! You're a leper! You're unclean!"

But Jesus did not move. Instead He stood there looking down in tender pity upon the poor sick man, now on his knees before Him.

"If You will, You can make me clean," cried the leper. And the cry came out of his heart.

Then what do you suppose Jesus did? He touched the leper, saying, "I will; be clean." He could have merely spoken to him, but He did more. He touched him.

The people around must have been shocked. They wouldn't have touched a leper for all the money in the Roman Empire. One touch might have made them lepers too. But Jesus was unafraid. Life poured from Him into the poor leper, making him whole. The very moment Jesus spoke "the leprosy departed from him, and he was cleansed."

Some time later, when Jesus was passing through Samaria, He came across ten lepers who "stood afar off," afraid to

come near Him. No doubt they had heard that He had healed other lepers, so they cried out at the top of their voices, "Jesus, Master, have mercy on us!" It was their one great chance for help, and they were not going to miss it.

Jesus heard their cry and turned toward them. His heart of love was saddened by their pitiful plight.

"Go show yourselves unto the priests," He called to them.

It was a strange thing for Him to say, but they understood. No leper could ever come back into society unless the priests said he was cured. So what Jesus had said meant they would be cured by the time they got to the priests.

They took Jesus at His word and started off. No doubt they kept looking at each other to see whether any change was taking place. And then it happened. Suddenly all the horrible white spots on them disappeared. Their half-rotted flesh

became clean and whole. Their spoiled features were restored just as they had been in days gone by.

"I'm healed!" cried one.

"So am I!" cried another.

"And I!" "And I!" cried the rest as they all began running to the nearest place where a priest might be found.

Jesus watched them go. Then to His great joy He saw one of them turn around and come running back to Him. Falling at Jesus' feet this man, a Samaritan, cried, "Thank You, dear Master, thank You!"

Jesus was pleased. It was good to find somebody so grateful.

Turning to the people standing by He said, "Were there not ten cleansed? but where are the nine?" Why didn't *they* come back and say "Thank you" too?

It just shows that Jesus notices things like this. Let us be sure that we thank Him for all His goodness to us.

STORY 10

Hungry People Fed

O NE MORNING Ben had been down to the lake with his fishing pole and caught two little fish.

"Look, Mother!" he cried as he rushed into the kitchen, "See what I caught!"

Mother looked and smiled. "They're not very big, are they?" she said. "What are you going to do with them?"

"They'll do for my lunch, if you'll cook them for me."

"Lunch? What are you planning to do today?"

"Oh, I'm going to listen to Jesus again. He's wonderful. You should go and hear Him too. Could I have three or four of the little barley loaves, Mother?"

"All right, dear. Take five. You'll be hungry before the day's over."

"Oh, thank you, Mother," cried Ben, and in a little while he was on his way.

There was no trouble finding Jesus. Everybody seemed to know where He was. On the main road, across the fields, along the mountain trails, hundreds of excited people in small and large groups were going in the same direction.

By and by the crowd got more and more dense. Ben had never seen so many people before. He pressed through, squeezing this way and that so he could get in front and be near the great Teacher.

Soon Jesus began to talk. And He said such beautiful things in such a kind and gentle way that the people loved every word. He spoke so clearly that even those farthest away could hear what He said.

Hour after hour slipped by, and still He talked. And still the people listened. They were so interested that they forgot all about eating. Ben even forgot to eat his lunch.

By and by the sun began to sink and a chilly breeze blew up from the lake.

"Don't You think it's time to send the people home?" one of the disciples said to Jesus.

"At least let's tell them to go and buy food in the villages around," said another. "They haven't eaten all day."

"They don't need to go," said Jesus; "you feed them."

The disciples were shocked. "*We* don't have any food," they said.

"Two hundred pennyworth wouldn't be enough to feed all this crowd," said Philip; "even if everyone had only a little."

Ben heard them talking and wondered what it was all about. It could be that Jesus was hungry; and no wonder, after talking all day. Then he thought about his lunch.

42

HUNGRY PEOPLE FED

"If the Master's hungry," he said to Andrew, who was standing by, "He may have my lunch."

Andrew smiled and spoke to Jesus.

"There's a lad here," he said, "who has five barley loaves and two small fishes. But what are they among so many?"

"Tell everybody to sit down," said Jesus. And they did.

"Sit down! Sit down everybody!" the disciples shouted, moving out among the crowd.

"Why, what's the matter?" the people asked.

"We're going to eat."

"Eat? Why, where's the food?"

"Never mind. You'll see."

And now Ben was handing his lunch to Jesus, and Jesus was smiling at him and saying, "Thank you, Ben; thank you very much."

That sweet smile was worth everything to Ben. It more than made up for going without his lunch.

But he didn't lose his lunch, after all. Soon something very wonderful began to happen. First, Jesus blessed the bread and the two little fish. Then He began to break them into pieces and give them to His disciples. And the strange thing was, no matter how much He broke off, there was always some left.

Pretty soon all the disciples were carrying food to the people as fast as they could walk up and down that mountainside. Time and again they came back for more and there was always more bread and more fish waiting for them as it fell from the Master's hands.

Ben looked on amazed. He couldn't understand it. And I wouldn't be surprised if, every now and then, Jesus turned and gave him some food, just for himself. Never had he had so much to eat. He had far, far more than he would have had had he eaten his lunch all by himself.

HUNGRY PEOPLE FED

The Bible says that five thousand men were fed that afternoon, besides women and children. And everybody had all he could eat. In fact, when it was all over, Jesus said to His disciples, "Gather up the fragments that remain, that nothing be lost." Twelve baskets were filled, so greatly had everybody been blessed.

But there's something else very special about this story. It is found in John 6:6, where we are told that Jesus "knew what He would do." This means that, right from the start, when the people began to get hungry and the disciples started to worry about how much the food would cost, Jesus had everything planned. He knew about Ben. He knew about Ben's lunch. And He knew what He would do with it if Ben would give it to Him.

He had watched Ben all day. He had seen how interested he was. He knew Ben wanted to do something for Him. And so He planned the whole marvelous miracle with this little boy in mind!

Today He has His eye on YOU. Perhaps, who can tell, He is planning to do something great and wonderful with you. He knows what He would do if you would let Him, if you would place your best, your dearest treasure, in His hands.

STORY 11

Drowning Man Saved

FEEDING all those people must have put a great strain on Jesus and His disciples. In fact, the disciples were so weary after carrying all that food to the five thousand people that Jesus told them to get in a boat and sail to the other side of the lake for a rest.

Meanwhile He tried to send the people home. It was difficult, for some of them wanted to make Him a king then and there. A man who could provide free meals like this was the very person they were looking for to be the king of Israel. But Jesus did not want to be that sort of king, so He told them to leave Him alone. At last, after much coaxing they went away. Then He climbed the mountain again and prayed.

Later that night a storm came up. Remembering His disciples out on the lake, Jesus decided to go to them. So He went down to the shore and kept right on walking across the water. How He did it, nobody knows, but walk on the lake He did, for all the disciples saw Him.

47

INTING BY RUSSELL HARLAN   © 1956, BY REVIEW AND HERALD

en Peter saw Jesus walking on the water,
:epped boldly out of the boat to meet Him,
when he got his eyes off the Saviour, and
himself sinking, he cried, "Lord, save me!"

And were they scared! "It's a ghost!" they cried as the white form of the Master appeared, gliding gently over the crested waves.

"It is I; be not afraid," Jesus called to them.

They couldn't believe their ears or their eyes. How could Jesus be out there on the water with no boat under Him?

Always ready with a bright idea, Peter called out, "Lord, if it's really You, tell me to come to You on the water."

"Come!" said Jesus.

Probably Peter didn't expect such an answer. But now he clambered over the side of the boat and started to go to his beloved Master. That took a lot of courage on such a dark night and a rough lake. But Peter was well rewarded.

This was wonderful! He was actually walking on water, just as Jesus was. He hadn't thought it possible. Why hadn't he tried it before?

But his joy and courage didn't last long. Taking his eyes off Jesus, he began to look around at the waves. What if one of them should knock him over? What if he couldn't keep his footing? He began to doubt. And that very moment he began to sink.

"Lord, save me!" he cried.

In a flash Jesus was by his side, holding him up.

"O you of little faith," He said, "why did you doubt?"

As the two stepped over the side of the boat the sea suddenly became calm. So did the disciples. Remembering the miracle of yesterday, and now this, they fell on their knees before Him crying, "Of a truth Thou art the Son of God!"

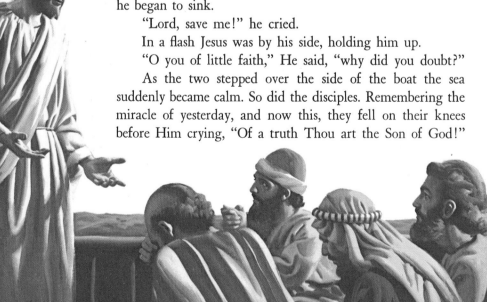

STORY 12

Greedy Man Made Generous

NOT ONLY did Jesus heal the sick, cleanse lepers, restore cripples, open the eyes of the blind, make the deaf hear, feed the hungry, save the drowning, and raise the dead, but He somehow got right inside people's minds and hearts and made them think and act like new men and women. He was indeed the Prince of healers.

Coming out of Jericho one day with a great company of people about Him, His keen eyes caught sight of a very short man running ahead of the crowd. It was Zacchaeus, the chief tax collector of the district and very rich.

Zacchaeus ran on till he got to a sycamore tree. There, forgetting his importance, he climbed the tree like a boy and made himself comfortable in the branches.

Jesus was glad that such a man as this was interested enough to go to all this trouble just to catch a glimpse of Him as He passed by.

The crowd moved slowly on, with some people shoving

hard to get closer to Jesus and others calling loudly to Him for help.

At the sycamore tree Jesus stopped and looked up into the face of Zacchaeus.

The tax collector was delighted. Here was the great Teacher of Galilee right underneath him, looking up at him —yes, smiling at him!

Something began to happen inside him then and there. Surely, he thought, Jesus couldn't be interested in *him*. Not in a tax collector. Everybody hated tax collectors.

But Jesus *was* interested in him. Very much so.

Then, to the surprise of Zacchaeus and everybody else around, Jesus said, "Zacchaeus, hurry up and come down. I want to stay in your house today."

"My house?" asked Zacchaeus, his eyes opening wide in surprise and a smile wreathing his face. "My house?"

The next moment he had slid down the tree and was standing beside Jesus.

"Do come! You are so welcome," he said, and proudly led Jesus to his home.

The people in the crowd couldn't understand it. They began to complain that Jesus had left them to go off with a tax collector, of all people!

But Jesus knew what He was doing. He could see all the hidden good in this little man, good that was waiting just for love to bring it out.

It was a fine house they went into, one of the best on the outskirts of Jericho. No doubt it had a beautiful view over the Jordan valley.

Zacchaeus ordered his servants to bring cool drinks and the best of food for his Guest, so pleased was he that the great Teacher had been willing to come to his home.

I wish I knew all that Jesus said to Zacchaeus as they sat together in the living room, or maybe on the porch that day. But I don't. Nobody does. All we know is that before the afternoon was over, Zacchaeus was a changed man.

"Jesus," he said, "I've made up my mind. I'm going to give half of all I own to the poor. And if I've ever taken any

money from anybody unlawfully, I'm going to give it back four times over."

Jesus was delighted. "This day is salvation come to this house," He said.

Then He uttered those words that have brought so much blessing to millions of people ever since: "For the Son of man is come to seek and to save that which was lost."

Yes. Rich and poor. High and low. Sick and well. Old and young. The tax collector and those who are taxed. Anybody who is lost, who wants to find the way home to God and heaven, may know that Jesus is seeking him and will save him if he wants to be saved.

Dear boy or girl, wherever you are—up a tree, in a boat, on a city street, or in your own little bedroom—Jesus is looking for you.

PART II

Stories of the Prince of Teachers

(MATTHEW 5:1-7:27; 17:1-18:35; 20:20-28; MARK 7:
1-23; 10:32-40; LUKE 6:1-49; 9:28-42; 10:38-14:6)

STORY 1

Secrets of Happiness

JESUS was not only the Prince of healers; He was the Prince of teachers, too. He had something on His heart that He wanted to tell people, and He told it so simply and clearly that they loved every word. They listened to Him just as long as He would talk to them.

He had come from heaven to tell them about God. He wanted them to know that God is a God of love; that He is kind, patient, and forgiving, yet at the same time a holy God who expects His children to be good, pure, truthful, and obedient.

He talked much about His coming kingdom and what a happy place it would be—a place where everybody would love everybody else and nobody would ever do anything wrong, unkind, or mean.

Anybody, just anybody, could belong to His kingdom, just as long as he believed in Jesus and was willing to do as He said. And he didn't have to wait a long, long time to

55

PAINTING BY HERBERT RUDEEN   © 1956, BY REVIEW AND HERALD

the people sat around Jesus on the hillside,
told them of His coming kingdom and of
home being prepared for those redeemed
ugh faith in His sacrifice on Calvary.

enjoy the happiness of that kingdom. He could have it now.

Certain of God's love, sure of His watchcare, the believer in Jesus could live without a single care or worry, his heart forever bubbling over with joy and peace.

This is what Jesus meant when, sitting on the mountainside one day, He said to the people who were sitting all around Him:

"Blessed are the poor in spirit: for their's is the kingdom of heaven.

"Blessed are they that mourn: for they shall be comforted.

"Blessed are the meek: for they shall inherit the earth.

"Blessed are they which do hunger and thirst after righteousness: for they shall be filled.

"Blessed are the merciful: for they shall obtain mercy.

"Blessed are the pure in heart: for they shall see God.

"Blessed are the peacemakers: for they shall be called the children of God.

"Blessed are they which are persecuted for righteousness' sake: for their's is the kingdom of heaven.

"Blessed are ye, when men shall revile you, and persecute you, and shall say all manner of evil against you falsely, for My sake.

"Rejoice, and be exceeding glad: for great is your reward in heaven: for so persecuted they the prophets which were before you."

In these wonderful words Jesus told the secrets of true

happiness. To be blessed, to be truly happy, He said, depends on how we live before God.

If we—you and I—keep humble, and never let pride come into our hearts, the kingdom of heaven will be ours—not only in the future, but now.

If we are truly sorry for our sins, and "mourn" for them because they offend God, He will comfort us with His forgiveness.

If with all our hearts we long to be good, God will bless our lives with victory over all temptations.

If we are kind and merciful to others, we shall have the joy of seeing them merciful to us.

If we keep our hearts pure and refuse to think evil thoughts, our minds will be clear to understand God, and great will be the happiness that will bring.

If we try to be peacemakers, loving others instead of fighting them, all sorts of blessings will be ours; but, best of all, we shall know for sure that we are the children of God.

If we get into trouble for doing right, and are misunderstood for following God's way, we need not worry. All will come right in the end. His kingdom is ours, now and forever.

We can even be happy when people try to do us harm. No matter how mean they become, we can "rejoice, and be exceeding glad," for God knows all about it and is saving up a great reward for us in heaven.

STORY 2

Lessons From Little Things

M OST of the people who came to listen to Jesus had never been to school. Many of them could not read or write.

In the crowds that followed Him were some priests and Levites and a few well-to-do people who had been to the schools of the rabbis, but the farmers, the cattlemen, the shepherds, the vineyard workers, the stonemasons, the carpenters, and the housewives knew very little beyond what they had been told by their parents or had heard in the synagogues from Sabbath to Sabbath.

That is why Jesus made His teaching so simple, and why "the common people heard Him gladly."

He talked about salt and candles, baskets and flowers, pigs and pearls, seeds and weeds, grapes and figs, sparrows and eagles, narrow gates and wide gates; and from these simple, everyday things He drew some of His biggest lessons.

There was much salt in the Jordan valley. From where

they were sitting, perhaps the people could see it gleaming white in the sunshine—and they all knew it was used to make things taste better, and to preserve them. So Jesus said, in other words, "You should be like that. God wants you to be the salt of the earth, making life happier for others, setting them a good example, standing always for the right."

Everybody knew what Jesus meant when He spoke of a lamp or a candle. That's all the light they had in their homes, for of course there was no electricity or gas in those days. And when Jesus asked them if, when they lighted a lamp, they covered it with a basket, I can imagine they all smiled and said, "Of course we don't!"

"Surely," said Jesus. "You put it on a stand so that it will light your house." Then He added, "Let your light so shine before men, that they may see your good works, and glorify your Father which is in heaven."

They got His point. They were to *be* good and *do* good, not to glorify themselves but God. Thus their goodness would shine like a light in the dark, and they would be the "light of the world."

A little later on He called attention to the birds that were flying around.

"Look at them," He said. "They don't sow seed; they don't reap harvests; they don't gather grain into barns; yet your heavenly Father feeds them. So why worry so? Aren't you much better than they?"

Then He pointed to the flowers growing at His feet on the mountainside. "Consider the lilies of the field," He said, "how they grow; they toil not, neither do they spin: and yet I say unto you, That even Solomon in all his glory was not arrayed like one of these."

Then came this lesson: "Wherefore, if God so clothe the grass of the field, . . . shall He not much more clothe you, O ye of little faith?"

He was trying to take all needless cares and worries out of their lives, for people worried just as much in those days as they do now.

They were not to keep on saying, "What shall we eat? or, What shall we drink? or, Wherewithal shall we be clothed?"

And why? Because, Jesus said, "Your heavenly Father knows you need all these things."

That is what He was trying to tell them. Trust God! He loves you! He is thinking about you, caring for you, planning for you! If they would but seek first the kingdom of God and His righteousness, "all these things" would be given them.

"Just suppose," He said, "that your son asked you for a piece of bread—would you give him a stone?"

"No!" answered the crowd.

"Well, if he asked you for a fish, would you give him a snake?"

"No!" cried the crowd again.

"Well, if you know how to give good gifts to *your* children, how much more shall your Father which is in heaven give good things to them that ask Him?"

Here again He was helping them to understand the love of God.

"Ask, and it shall be given you;" He urged them, "seek, and ye shall find; knock, and it shall be opened unto you."

Heaven was that close! They could knock on the door and it would open!

HERBERT RUDEEN

STORY 3

God's Better Way

A S JESUS talked to the people He seemed to be saying, "I know a better way for you to live. And if you will try to live My way—God's way—you will be so much happier."

His way, of course, was the way of love. See how He tried to make it plain to those who came to listen to Him:

"Ye have heard," He said, "that it was said by them of old time, Thou shalt not kill; and whosoever shall kill shall be in danger of the judgment: but I say unto you, That whosoever is angry with his brother . . . shall be in danger of the judgment."

Here was a new idea. It was not only wrong to kill but wrong even to be angry. In fact, Jesus said, just calling your brother a fool is displeasing to God. And why? Because it isn't the way of love.

Love is kind, gentle, polite, forgiving. Boys and girls with love in their hearts will never say or do mean things to other children, but will do and say things to make them happy.

Again, Jesus said, "Ye have heard that it hath been said by them of old time, Thou shalt not forswear thyself . . . : but I say unto you, Swear not at all; neither by heaven; for it is God's throne: nor by the earth; for it is His footstool: neither by Jerusalem; for it is the city of the great King."

Here was another new idea. The people knew that it was wrong to swear falsely, but it had never occurred to them that God might be just as displeased with ordinary foolish swearing. But He is, said Jesus, and those who love Him with all their hearts will never take His name in vain like this.

Now Jesus brought out yet another new idea—and a very startling one it was, too.

"Ye have heard that it hath been said, An eye for an eye, and a tooth for a tooth: but I say unto you, That ye resist not evil: but whosoever shall smite thee on thy right cheek, turn

to him the other also. And if any man will sue thee at the law, and take away thy coat, let him have thy cloke also. And whosoever shall compel thee to go a mile, go with him twain."

This was hard to take. No doubt many in the crowd were thinking, "If I could just get hold of so-and-so, I'd treat him as he treated me"; but now they knew they must never think such thoughts again. God's better way was the way of forgiveness, of "turning the other cheek," of "giving the cloke with the coat," and of "going the second mile."

But now Jesus went still further, saying,

"Ye have heard that it hath been said, Thou shalt love thy neighbour, and hate thine enemy. But I say unto you, Love your enemies, bless them that curse you, do good to them that hate you, and pray for them which despitefully use you, and persecute you; that ye may be the children of your Father which is in heaven."

"What!" I can hear someone asking, "Do you mean to say we are to love the Romans, the tax collectors, and everybody else who tries to rob us and do us harm?"

"Yes," said Jesus, "Everybody. Just as the sun shines on

the good and the evil and the rain falls on the just and the unjust, so you are to radiate love to friend and enemy alike."

Some thought that Jesus was trying to do away with all the old laws they had heard about in the synagogue.

"Oh, no," He said; "don't think I am come to destroy the law, or the prophets: I am not come to destroy, but to fulfill."

There was nothing the matter with the law; it was the way they were trying to keep it that was wrong. The only way the law could ever be kept was in a spirit of love. If their hearts were full of love; if they loved God with all their mind and soul and strength; and if they loved their neighbors as much as they loved themselves; they would fulfill all the law asked of them.

It was love that mattered most to God. This was His better way, the way to real, lasting happiness.

We must try to follow this better way today.

8-5

STORY 4

How to Pray

MANY of the people who listened to Jesus did not know how to pray. Some of them had never prayed in all their lives.

This was the cause of their sorrows, their worries, their failures. Jesus knew that. So He tried to get them to think of God as their Friend and to talk to Him as to one who loved them and was interested in them.

How could they live the good life and walk God's better way if they never asked Him for help?

Jesus prayed much Himself. Sometimes He would spend a whole night in prayer, talking with His heavenly Father and seeking help for the great work He had come to the earth to do.

Once when He looked up from praying He found some of His disciples standing by, watching Him. They had been listening to His simple, beautiful words as He talked with His Father, and they wished they could pray like that.

HOW TO PRAY

"Lord, teach us to pray," they said, and Jesus was pleased. He had hoped that they would ask that question. Now He could tell them the secret of prayer and they would listen and remember.

First of all, He said, they should not pray just so other people would think they were good and pious. Long, loud prayers in public to be "seen of men" aren't prayers at all. They don't reach heaven. God doesn't hear them.

"When you pray," He said, "go into your room and shut the door." Prayer is something very private, just between you and God.

And "when you pray," He said, "use not vain repetitions, as the heathen do." Don't feel you must keep saying the same words over and over. Just talk as you would to a friend.

Then He taught them the little prayer that has become known to millions upon millions of people all over the world as the Lord's Prayer.

Our Father which art in heaven, Hallowed be thy name. Thy kingdom come. Thy will be done in earth, as it is in heaven. Give us this day our daily bread. And forgive us our debts, as we forgive our debtors. And lead us not into temptation, but deliver us from evil: For thine is the kingdom, and the power, and the glory, for ever. Amen.

HOW TO PRAY

From the first word to the last it is the perfect prayer. It turns our thoughts heavenward. It makes us think of God. His holiness. His kingdom. His power. His glory. And all it asks for ourselves is our daily bread, a forgiving spirit, and strength to overcome evil.

There is not a single selfish request, for even those that mention our needs are for the glory of God and the helping forward of His plans for His kingdom of love.

We should learn this prayer and say it often. Yet it is not the only prayer we should pray. For God is our Friend, and He wants us to tell Him all that is in our hearts. How much we love Him; how earnestly we want to please Him; how much we need His help to do what is good and true and right; and how eagerly we want to serve Him all the days of our lives.

STORY 5

Treasures in Heaven

I N THOSE far-off days when Jesus was teaching in Galilee there were no banks such as are to be found in every city today. If a man had something of value he wanted to keep very safely he put it in a hole in the ground, or in a cellar under his house.

But the best of such hiding places were not very safe. If they were damp, then the precious object became rusty or tarnished. If they were dry, and the treasure was a beautiful garment, or a priceless picture, or a valuable piece of furniture, then moths or worms or white ants would destroy it. Then, too, there was always the danger that thieves might break in and steal it, or an invading army carry it away.

There simply wasn't any safety anywhere, and Jesus pointed out to the people how foolish it was of them to spend so much time saving money to buy things that wouldn't last, or that couldn't be kept very long, or that could be so easily stolen.

TREASURES IN HEAVEN

"Lay not up for yourselves treasures upon earth, where moth and rust . . . corrupt, and where thieves break through and steal," He said: "but lay up for yourselves treasures in heaven."

Such treasures would be safe forever. No moths, no rust, no thieves, can get in there.

The people must have looked at Him with a puzzled expression on their faces. What did He mean? How could anybody put treasures in heaven?

Perhaps somebody called out, "You mean I can put my money in heaven and it will be safe from robbers?"

"Yes."

"But how?"

"By giving it to somebody in need."

Then everybody must have smiled. It seemed so foolish. Yet it wasn't. It was very, very true. Because, you see, when we use our treasure in a spirit of love to help others we really give it to God; and God, who never forgets a single good deed done in His name, in some way will repay our gift,

and often it is much more than we could ever wish for.

"Give, and it shall be given unto you," said Jesus; "good measure, pressed down, and shaken together, and running over, shall men give into your bosom. For with the same measure that ye mete withal it shall be measured to you again."

Love puts the treasure in heaven and love pays it out again.

Of course it takes faith to put money—or anything else—into this kind of bank. But it takes faith to put money in any kind of bank, doesn't it? Of course it does! Even a piggy bank!

So to make this new kind of banking work, you have to believe in God, and heaven, and love—which is the only kind of money heaven knows.

"Where your treasure is," said Jesus, "there will your heart be also." If your treasure is in your basement, or anywhere else on earth, you'll be forever worrying about it; but if you use it in love to the glory of God you will put it in heaven; and your heart, following it there, will find the peace and happiness which heaven alone can give.

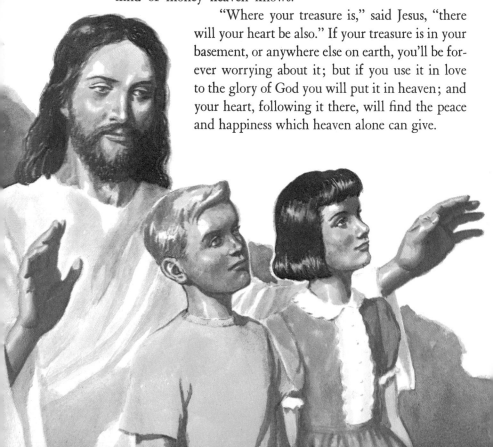

STORY 6

House on a Rock

A S JESUS came to the end of His long sermon about the love of God He drew another striking picture, which was so simple and clear that everybody understood it at once.

It was a picture of two houses—one built on rock, the other on sand. Both looked alike: both seemed good to live in. But a storm came up and a flash flood filled the river bed. One house stood; the other fell and was swept away.

Everybody listening to Him, Jesus said, was building on one kind of foundation or the other.

Those who made up their minds to follow His teaching and let the love of God fill their hearts and rule their lives, were like the man who "digged deep, and laid the foundation on a rock."

On the other hand, those who refused to heed His teachings and decided to go on living the same old kind of life, with all its meanness and littleness, were like the man who

73

had "without a foundation built an house upon the earth."

In the days ahead fierce storms would blow upon all their houses. Great floods of trial would come to them. And in that time of testing the kind of foundation they had built upon would be revealed.

Nothing will ever hurt the man who builds his life on love, for love—though it cannot be seen or felt—is like a rock. It lasts. It is eternal, like God Himself. The person who loves greatly, who lives not for himself but for others, becomes so wrapped up in God's plans for the future that he just goes on with God forever and ever.

On the other hand, the shallow little person, who thinks only of himself, cannot endure trial. He goes all to pieces. He has no future, for he has no love.

On what are you planning to build your house? On sand? Or on rock?

If you want it to stand forever, dig deep. The rock is there.

STORY 7

Good Deeds on a Good Day

T HE MORE Jesus talked about His kingdom of love the more He seemed to get into trouble with the religious leaders of His day.

Because He said that loving people and being kind to them was more important than all the rules of conduct anybody ever made they said He was a rebel. They spread the story that He was against all religion because He was against *their kind* of religion. And oh, how they watched Him to see if He would break another of their rules!

One Sabbath day Jesus walked through the grainfields with His disciples. Being hungry, they plucked some ears of grain, rubbed them in their hands, and ate the kernels.

"Sabbathbreakers!" muttered some Pharisees who were looking on. To them this was as bad as harvesting the whole grainfield on the Sabbath.

"Why are you doing what is not lawful on the Sabbath?" they demanded.

But Jesus was ready for them.

"Haven't you read about David?" He said, reminding them of the time when, fleeing from Saul, David went into the tabernacle and ate the holy shewbread, giving some to those who were with him.

The Pharisees remembered all right, and they didn't know what to say about it. So Jesus said to them, "The Son of man is Lord of the Sabbath."

This must have shocked them greatly, for it was as if He had said, "I made the Sabbath, and I am the One to say how it should be kept."

If it had been wrong for the disciples to pluck those ears of grain on the Sabbath, Jesus would have said so; but to Him

76

it wasn't wrong. They weren't *working,* but getting necessary food in a very simple way, just as you eat your breakfast or lunch on the Sabbath today.

The same question came up over and over again. On another Sabbath as Jesus was speaking in a synagogue, He noticed a poor woman all doubled up from some terrible disease. She had been like this for eighteen years, and nobody had ever been able to help her.

Touching her gently, He said, "Woman, you are free from your sickness."

At once she stood up straight, her face radiant with joy and gratitude. But the ruler of the synagogue was furious. Turning to the people about him, he said, "There are six days in which men ought to work: in them therefore come and be healed, and not on the Sabbath day."

Jesus looked around. "You hypocrites!" He said sternly. "Doth not each one of you on the Sabbath loose his ox or his ass from the stall, and lead him away to watering? And ought not this woman, being a daughter of Abraham, whom Satan hath bound, lo, these eighteen years, be loosed from this bond on the Sabbath day?"

At this those who opposed Him were ashamed, as well they should have been. But the rest "rejoiced for all the glorious things that were done by Him."

On yet another Sabbath, when dining in the home of one of the chief Pharisees, Jesus noticed that one of the men present had dropsy. So He asked the Pharisees and lawyers who were there, "Is it lawful to heal on the Sabbath?"

They didn't answer. So He healed the man on the spot. Then He asked another question: "Which of you shall have an ass or an ox fallen into a pit, and will not straightway pull him out on the Sabbath day?"

Again nobody answered.

Perhaps Jesus looked all along the row of puzzled, angry faces, as if saying, "Well, how about you?—and you?—and you?"

Of course they would help their animals on the Sabbath! Some of them had done it many times. Yet they thought it was a sin to heal a poor sick man! How mixed up they all were!

Of course it is right to do good on the Sabbath day. As Jesus said time and again, "The Sabbath was made for man"—for his good, his happiness, his welfare—"and not man for the Sabbath."

STORY   8

Glimpse of the Kingdom

ONE DAY Jesus said a very strange thing to His disciples: "There be some standing here, which shall not taste of death, till they see the Son of man coming in His kingdom."

You can imagine how they must have looked at each other, wondering what He meant and who the favored ones would be.

Did He mean that before all the disciples should die He would begin His reign as King of love in all the world? If so, how wonderful!

But Jesus didn't mean that at all. He had something else in mind.

As it turned out, the favored ones were Peter, James, and John. Jesus took them off by themselves and led them up a high mountain, possibly Mount Hermon, which is almost always snow capped.

Up, up, up the steep slope they followed their beloved

79

Master till all were weary with the climb. When at last, near the summit, Jesus stopped, they were ready to lie down and sleep. In fact, their eyes were so "heavy with sleep" that they almost missed the most wonderful sight that human eyes ever saw.

They had often seen Jesus praying before, but never like this! His face was glowing with a glorious, heavenly light. His garments were glistening as when the sun shines upon purest snow. He looked like a king—but more than a king. Yes, He looked like God!

Then they saw something else that startled them. From nowhere, it seemed, two strangers appeared and stood by Jesus.

The disciples stared at them. Could they be angels? No. They were men all right. There was no doubt about that. But who were they? And how had they come so suddenly upon this mountaintop?

The disciples had no way of knowing who these two people might be, nor had they seen any likeness of them at any time. But Jesus knew them and talked with them as if they were old friends of His, as indeed they were.

One was Moses; the other was Elijah.

But weren't these two people dead?

No. After Moses died on Mount Nebo, God raised him from the dead, as we understand from the book of Jude.

As for Elijah, he never died, but was taken to heaven in a chariot of fire.

So here on this mountaintop Jesus gave His three most trusted disciples a picture of what is going to happen in that

8-6

ldenly while Peter, James, and John prayed
he mountainside with Jesus, He was envel-
d with the dazzling light of heaven, and two
1, Moses and Elijah, appeared at His side.

glorious day when He will return to set up His kingdom.

On that happy morning He will appear in all His glory as King of kings and Lord of lords. Then all who have died believing in Him will be raised to life—as Moses was; and those still living will be caught up in the clouds to meet Him in the air, like Elijah.

After a little while Moses and Elijah vanished. When they were gone Peter said to Jesus, "Let us make three booths, one for You, one for Moses, and one for Elijah."

It was a foolish thing to say at such a time. In very sacred moments like this it is always good to keep quiet and say nothing.

Jesus did not answer. And a moment later a cloud came down and covered Him. Presently from the cloud came a voice, rich, beautiful, and full of melody, and it said, "This is My beloved Son, in whom I am well pleased; hear ye Him."

Thus again God claimed Jesus as His Son, as He had done once before by the Jordan.

Terrified, the three disciples fell on their faces. How long they stayed like this we do not know, but by and by each felt a familiar touch on the shoulder: "Get up," said Jesus gently. "Don't be afraid."

They looked up and "saw Jesus only."

Why did Jesus let Peter, James, and John have this wonderful experience?

Because He knew they would need it in the sad, trying years ahead. It would help to keep up their courage when His cause would appear to be lost and everything would seem to go wrong.

The Prince of teachers was right. The disciples never forgot that marvelous sight on the mountain.

Long years afterward Peter wrote about it saying, "We . . . were eyewitnesses of His majesty."

And John, in the first chapter of his Gospel, said, "We beheld His glory, the glory as of the only begotten of the Father." For the rest of their lives this was one of their most precious and sacred memories.

STORY 9

Why the Power Failed

ALAS, when the four reached the foot of the mountain again they didn't find any glory there.

Instead they found the other disciples in a very sad plight. They had met their first failure and didn't know what to do about it.

You see, a little while before this, Jesus had called His twelve disciples together and had given them power "over all devils, and to cure diseases." Then He had sent them out "to preach the kingdom of God, and to heal the sick."

At first they had been very happy about this. Indeed, they were thrilled to find that they were able to perform miracles of healing just as their Master did. And when they found that even the devils were subject unto them their joy knew no bounds.

This was wonderful! Humble fishermen from Galilee commanding demons to come out of people, and the demons doing as they were told!

84

WHY THE POWER FAILED

Day after day the miracles continued, with the disciples becoming bolder and bolder as they traveled about the country, bringing health and happiness to the needy.

Then came the sad day when all of a sudden the power didn't work any more. They found themselves as helpless as the people they were trying to heal.

A man had brought his demon-possessed son for healing, and the disciples commanded the evil spirit to leave the boy—but nothing happened. They tried again and again and still nothing happened. The boy raved on, completely crazy.

The poor father was bitterly disappointed. So were the disciples. What was the matter? they wondered. What had gone wrong? Why didn't the power of God work in this case?

About this time some of the people in the crowd caught sight of Jesus, with Peter, James, and John, coming down the mountain.

"There He is!" they cried. "He'll know what to do!" And, of course, He did.

The boy's father began to run toward Jesus, so anxious was he to get help for his boy.

"Master, I beseech Thee, look upon my son: for he is mine only child," he cried.

Then he told Jesus all about the boy: how the demons would throw him into the fire or into water; and there was nothing anybody could do for him. Not even the disciples.

"I begged Your disciples to cast out the devil," he said, "but they couldn't."

"Bring him to Me," said Jesus.

The father took the boy's hand and tried to lead him over to where Jesus was standing; but at that very moment the boy fell on the ground in a fit.

Jesus took one look at the pitiful sight, then commanded the demon to come out of him.

The demon obeyed, and the boy "was cured from that very hour."

Those who saw the miracle marveled "at the mighty power of God"; but the disciples were very much upset. Jesus had succeeded where they had failed, and they were ashamed.

WHY THE POWER FAILED

What *was* the matter? they kept asking themselves. Had they said the wrong words, or what?

When everybody else had gone away they came to Jesus and asked Him, "Why could not we cast him out?"

"Because of your unbelief," said Jesus.

If only they had just a teeny-weeny bit of faith—as small as a grain of mustard seed—He told them, they would be able to say to a whole mountain of trouble, "Go away!" and it would go. Nothing would be impossible for them.

Wouldn't it be wonderful to have faith like this and be able to do "impossible" things for God? It would indeed. And you may have it, if you wish.

But, remember, this kind of faith comes only, as Jesus said, "by prayer and fasting." That is, you have to want it very, very much, with all your heart. And you must want it for God's glory, not yours.

The real trouble with the disciples that day was that they had been arguing among themselves as to which of them was the greatest. I wouldn't be surprised if they had been adding up the miracles God had wrought through each of them and comparing one with another to see who had done the most!

No wonder the power had stopped flowing! No wonder the devil had got the best of them! No wonder their faith had shriveled up till it was so small God couldn't find enough of it to use to save this one poor demon-possessed boy!

The channels of our hearts must be clear of all pride, all selfishness, all vainglory, before the power of God can flow through them in all its fullness.

STORY 10

Money in a Fish

E VEN though Jesus tried His best to love people and
be kind to them, there were always some men around
Him who didn't want to be loved. They disliked Him
because He was so popular and hated Him because He was
so good.

It happens like that at school sometimes. The bad boys
"take it out" on those who behave themselves, and the slackers
are mean to the ones who study hard and get good grades.

Jesus' enemies were forever trying to trick Him into saying or doing something that would get Him into trouble.

One day a group came to Him and, trying to appear very
innocent, asked, "Is it lawful to pay tribute to Caesar?"

Jesus saw the trap at once. If He said No, the Romans
would arrest Him for treason; if He said Yes, the people who
hated the Romans would have a case against Him.

So He didn't say Yes or No. He merely asked for a coin
and pointed to the face on it. "Whose image is this?" He asked.

MONEY IN A FISH

"Caesar's," they said, wondering at His question.

"Render therefore unto Caesar the things which are Caesar's," He replied; "and unto God the things that are God's."

This left them to decide which things belong to Caesar and which belong to God. This was too hard for them, so they "left Him, and went their way."

Another time the tax collectors in Capernaum asked Peter whether his Master paid tax.

"Yes," said Peter, hurrying home to tell Jesus what they had said to him.

It seems that the tax at that time was half a shekel, and Jesus, while willing to pay it, didn't have that much money. So He told Peter to do a very unusual thing.

"Lest we should offend them," He said, "go . . . to the

sea and cast." Jesus promised that the first fish he would catch would have a piece of money in its mouth.

Off Peter went with his line and hook. Though he had fished all his life this was the strangest fishing trip he had ever been on.

Arriving at the beach he baited the hook and threw it as far from the shore as he could. Then he waited. Presently there was a sharp tug. His line tightened. He pulled on it, then carefully hauled it in. Soon he could see a fish jumping and splashing about in the water.

"This must be it!" he said to himself. "The Master said it would be the first one."

Grabbing the fish in both hands, he forced its mouth open. Inside was one shekel, exactly the amount needed to pay the tax for both Jesus and himself!

STORY 11

Seventy Times Seven

D OES your brother, or your sister, tease you a lot? Do you feel sometimes that you cannot take any more?

What would Jesus do if He were in your place?

Let's ask the Prince of teachers and see what He says.

Listen: "If your brother sins, rebuke him, and if he repents, forgive him; and if he sins against you seven times in the day, and turns to you seven times, and says, 'I repent,' you must forgive him."

Seven times! you say. What a lot of times!

But no. When Peter came to Jesus and asked how many times he should forgive *his* brother, and whether seven times was the limit, Jesus said he was to go on forgiving him "until seventy times seven."

How many times is that? Four hundred and ninety!

Why, you say, I couldn't keep count of all those times. Of course you couldn't! And Jesus knew that perfectly well when He said it. He doesn't keep account of the number of times He forgives us.

Four hundred and ninety times would mean once a day for more than a year!

Have you ever tried forgiving anybody that many times? If not, and you are feeling angry with somebody right now, get a notebook and pencil and start writing. First, put down all the things this somebody has done to upset you. Next, write "forgiven" across the list. Then put a check mark beside that precious word every time you tell that person you forgive him when he annoys you again.

By the time you have made twenty or thirty check marks that somebody will probably be your best friend. Try it and see. Even the meanest people can't resist pure love like that.

Forgiving is part of God's better way, the way of love, which Jesus came from heaven to reveal to us.

SEVENTY TIMES SEVEN

Forgiving someone over and over again—fifty times, a hundred times, four hundred and ninety times—is love in action, love at its best and grandest, love reaching out to another heart with all its healing, winning power.

We can never hope to belong to Christ's kingdom of love if we do not know how to forgive people who do us wrong. He couldn't afford to let us in. We'd be having trouble with somebody in no time at all.

"Forgive us . . . as we forgive," we pray every time we say the Lord's Prayer. But how do we forgive? Just a little bit? Just once now and then? Just when we feel in the right mood? We wouldn't want God to forgive us like that.

No, Jesus wants us to be so full of His love that a forgiving spirit will come naturally. We will never take offense. No matter what anybody says or does to us, we will go on loving him just the same.

So important is it that we have this forgiving spirit in our hearts that Jesus said that if we take a gift to church and, on getting there, remember that a brother is upset with us for some reason or other, we are to forget the gift and find the brother. "*First* be reconciled to your brother, and then come and offer your gift," He said.

To Jesus, a loving, forgiving spirit is much more important than money. He would far rather we make peace with an old enemy than give a big donation to a church building fund.

So we had better start forgiving right away. Think! Is there someone *you* should forgive today?

STORY 12

Mrs. Zebedee's Mistake

THE BIBLE tells a good deal about the twelve disciples who followed Jesus, but it doesn't say much about their homes and families.

We know that Peter was married, for his "wife's mother" once had a fever and Jesus healed her.

But that's about all, except for Mrs. Zebedee, the mother of James and John. She at least got her name in print, if none of the others did. And that because of a dreadful mistake she made.

Like all mothers she was eager to see her children succeed. She wanted the best for her two precious boys, and there was nothing wrong about that.

When she heard that James and John were going about with the great Teacher of Galilee she was very glad, for she was sure He was a good man and would be a help to them.

As thousands flocked to Him, and it seemed certain that

MRS. ZEBEDEE'S MISTAKE

He would become king of Israel some day, a bright idea came to her. Next time she found Jesus alone she would whisper a word in His ear about her sons. Perhaps He hadn't noticed how very suitable they were to hold high positions in His coming kingdom. They were really outstanding, much better qualified than the others, and He should know about it in good time.

Her chance came at last.

Finding Jesus alone she went up to Him, with James and John, looking a bit sheepish no doubt, not far behind.

Kneeling, she told Jesus how much she thought of Him and His noble work, and how glad she was that He had chosen her two dear boys to be among His closest followers. She hoped they were giving Him all the help they should and,

well, there was just one thing she would like to mention.

"What do you want?" asked Jesus kindly.

Looking around to make sure no one was listening, she whispered, eagerly, "Grant that these my two sons may sit, the one on Thy right hand, and the other on the left, in Thy kingdom."

Jesus did not scold her. Perhaps He smiled at her, but there was sadness in His smile. He could see she did not in the least understand His kingdom nor what it was going to cost those who believed in it.

Turning to James and John, He asked them whether they thought they could share His future, whatever it might be.

"Oh, yes," they said eagerly. "We are able."

"You shall," said Jesus, "but to sit on My right hand, and on My left, is not Mine to give, but it shall be given to them for whom it is prepared of My Father."

A little later the whole story reached the ears of the other disciples. How, we don't know, but the best-kept secrets have a way of getting out.

The ten were angry. To think that Mrs. Zebedee would do a thing like this! they muttered to each other. Pushing her own children, that's what it was! Trying to cut the rest out! And they had worked just as hard, or harder, to set up the Master's kingdom.

Jesus knew what was going on. They couldn't have hidden their ugly thoughts from Him if they had tried. So He called them to Him and told them that it was time they all understood what kind of kingdom they were working for.

MRS. ZEBEDEE'S MISTAKE

In worldly kingdoms, He reminded them, rulers lord it over people, with big men bossing little men and demanding obedience: but this was not His way. In His kingdom love, and love alone, ruled. Love was the key to promotion and the chief offices were for those who served most humbly and unselfishly.

"Whosoever will be great among you, let him be your minister," He said; "and whosoever will be chief among you, let him be your servant: even as the Son of man came not to be ministered unto, but to minister, and to give His life a ransom for many."

Though many have forgotten what He said that day, this is still the way His kingdom is run—and will be, through all eternity.

STORY 13

Last Things Last

ARRIVING in the village of Bethany one day, Jesus knocked on the door of a humble' home.

"Come in and welcome!" said the bright-eyed, vigorous woman who opened the door.

It was Martha, and she was proud and glad that the famous Teacher of Galilee had come to her house to rest and eat.

"Mary!" I can hear her calling excitedly. "Mary! It's the Master. Hurry! Get the table laid! Fix the fire! Get that pot of beans boiling!"

At once the whole place was like a beehive, with Martha buzzing about at top speed doing all the things she thought should be done with such an important visitor in the house.

By and by a mixture of familiar sounds came from the kitchen. The clattering of pots and pans, the clink of dishes, the chop-chop-chop of a knife on wood, told that Martha was doing her utmost to give the Master the best meal she could.

Then after a long moment of silence, Martha shouted,

LAST THINGS LAST

"Mary! Where are you? Mary! I need you to stir the soup! Mary!"

Quick footsteps followed, all the way from the kitchen to the living room.

"Well, of all things!" cried Martha, as she caught sight of Mary sitting on the floor listening to Jesus.

Turning to her guest she said, rather testily, "Don't You care that my sister has left me to serve alone? Tell her to help me!"

Jesus looked at her, smiling gently as usual. "Martha, Martha," He said tenderly. "You are worried and troubled about many things; one thing is needful. Mary has chosen the good part which shall not be taken from her."

I don't think this means that Jesus did not appreciate all that Martha was doing. By no means. But He saw that

Martha needed to learn a very important spiritual lesson.

You see, Jesus was there for just one little day; perhaps for one brief hour. Martha saw in this a chance to cook and to make her house all spick and span for their honored Guest, but Mary saw in it her one great opportunity to talk with the Prince of teachers. Here He was, right in her own home. For all she knew then, it would never happen again.

There would always be the house to clean, dishes to wash, and food to cook, but this day, this wonderful day, Jesus was here. And there were so many questions she wanted to ask Him about His teachings and His kingdom. There wouldn't be time to ask them all, but while He was here she would make the most of every precious moment in His presence.

This was the "good part" that Mary chose. She could have chosen to sit on a kitchen stool and prepare vegetables, or mix a cheese omelet, but she chose instead to sit at Jesus' feet and learn of Him while she could.

Most of us need to make Mary's choice today. We are so much like Martha, rushing about at a terrible speed, clattering and banging our way through life, too busy to pray, too busy to read the Bible, too busy to go to church.

Of course we mustn't shirk our part of the humble, everyday duties. But let us try to put first things first and last things last, shall we?

And if we choose the good part, nobody will take it away from us. They couldn't. Not if we want it badly enough.

PART III

Stories of the Prince of Storytellers

(MATTHEW 13:1-50; 18:23-35; 21:28-22:14; MARK 12:1-44; LUKE 8:4-15; 10:25-37; 14:16-15:32; 18:9-14; 20:9-19)

STORY   1

Seeds of Love

T HE PRINCE of teachers was also the Prince of storytellers. Some of His most precious lessons were given
in true-to-life stories, which are sometimes called
parables.

One day, as He was talking to a great crowd of people
on the shores of Galilee, He tried to make them see why they
should listen carefully to what He was saying. He had come
to show them a new way of life, but if they would not listen,
or try to understand, it wouldn't do them any good.

As He spoke, in full view of everyone, a sower was going
about his lonely task in a nearby field. This gave Jesus the
idea for a story.

"A sower went forth to sow," He said; "and when he
sowed, some seeds fell by the way side, and the fowls came
and devoured them up: some fell upon stony places . . . ;
and when the sun was up, they were scorched. . . . And
some fell among thorns; and the thorns sprung up, and

103

AINTING BY RUSSELL HARLAN   © 1956, BY REVIEW AND HERALD

ng a sower in the fields Jesus taught them
rable; "A sower went forth to sow," He
; "and when he sowed, some seeds fell by
way side and the fowls . . . devoured them."

choked them: but others fell into good ground, and brought forth fruit, some an hundredfold, some sixtyfold, some thirty-fold."

The seed, He said later, was the word of God. So it could well be called the seed of love, for that was the word that Jesus had brought from God. "God loves you," He kept telling the people in various ways. "He loves you so much that He gave His only Son for you. In return He wants you to love Him and to love one another so you may belong to His kingdom of love."

This was the heart of His message, the wonderful "seed" He was scattering. But it would help none of them if they did not understand and believe it. So they must listen, and think, and study, and decide.

Some in the crowd had hearts as hard as the wayside. He knew that. The moment a seed of love lodged in their minds the devil would snatch it away.

Others would agree with His teaching and begin to put it into practice, but if someone laughed at them for doing so, they would give it up. The "heat" would be too much for them.

SEEDS OF LOVE

Then there were those who would follow the better way for a little while, but "the cares of this world, and the deceitfulness of riches" would choke their good resolutions as weeds choke good grain.

Some, however, not only would accept His message but would try to understand it. They would study it, and think about it, and pray about it. In so doing they would catch a vision of God's wonderful plan to save them, and this seed of love would produce a mighty harvest of good.

Simple as the story was, not everybody in the crowd caught its meaning. But some did. Here and there a man or woman, a boy or girl, said softly, "He's talking about me!"

He was. And as He scattered His seeds of love He hoped that they would fall into many such willing, friendly hearts and bring forth a "hundredfold" to the glory of God.

STORY 2

No Weeds in Heaven

LATER, in His great sermon by the sea, Jesus came back to His sower-and-seed idea. This time, however, He had a new lesson to teach; so He told the story in a different way.

A farmer, He said, sowed good seed in his field. The next night an enemy came and sowed tares, or weeds, in it.

When all the seeds began to grow the farmer noticed the weeds and said, "An enemy has done this."

His servants wanted to dig out the weeds right away, but the farmer wouldn't let them, in case they hurt the wheat too. "Let both grow together till the harvest," he said.

This was another very simple story, but it was full of deep meaning.

Jesus explained it like this: The farmer who sowed the good seed is "the Son of man"—Himself; "the field is the world; the good seed are the children of the kingdom; but the tares are the children of the wicked one; the enemy that

106

sowed them is the devil; the harvest is the end of the world; and the reapers are the angels.

"As therefore the tares are gathered and burned in the fire; so shall it be in the end of this world. The Son of man shall send forth His angels, and they shall gather out of His kingdom all things that offend, and them which do iniquity; and shall cast them into a furnace of fire."

This was a warning that many standing there that day had not expected. They had begun to think that if God loved the world as much as Jesus said He did, He would surely overlook every kind of sin and let everybody, no matter how bad, into His kingdom.

No, said Jesus. That isn't so. God will gladly forgive all who repent of their sins and turn in love to Him.

But where there's no repentance there can be no forgiveness. For those who refuse God's love and keep on sinning there is no hope. For them there is only the day of judgment, the harvest sifting, and the fire.

There will be no weeds in His kingdom.

STORY 3

The Good Samaritan

ONE DAY a lawyer came to Jesus and asked what seemed to be a very proper question.

"Master," he said, "what shall I do to inherit eternal life?"

Knowing that the man was only trying to start an argument, Jesus replied with another question, "What is written in the law?"

The lawyer answered, "Thou shalt love the Lord thy God with all thy heart, and with all thy soul, and with all thy strength, and with all thy mind; and thy neighbour as thyself."

"You have answered right," said Jesus. "Do this and you will live."

But the man was not satisfied.

"Who is my neighbor?" he asked; and this gave Jesus the chance to teach this man a lesson he greatly needed. And He did it by telling one of His most famous stories, a story that has been told and retold thousands of times since then.

"A certain man," said Jesus, "went down from Jerusalem to Jericho, and fell among thieves." These cutthroats wounded the lonely traveler, stole his clothes, and left him lying on the roadside half dead.

By chance a priest came by, but did not stop. He gave one glance at the wounded man and "passed by on the other side."

Next came a Levite. He at least took the trouble to go and look at the poor sufferer, but did nothing to help him. He, too, "passed by on the other side."

Then came a Samaritan—one of those people whom the Jews hated so much. When he saw what had happened he was filled with pity and, without a thought for himself, decided to do what he could to help.

Kneeling beside the injured man, he cleaned his wounds
as best he could and bound them up. Then, very carefully,
he placed him on his own donkey and took him to the nearest
inn. Here he got a room and food for him. The next day,
when he had to leave, he gave the innkeeper money and said,
"Take care of him, and if you spend more, I will pay you on
my return."

"Now," said Jesus, looking straight at the lawyer, "which
of these three, do you think, was neighbour to him who fell
among the thieves?"

"He who showed mercy on him," the lawyer replied.

"Go, and do likewise," said Jesus.

Whether the lawyer took Jesus' advice we do not know. If he didn't, then he will never enjoy the eternal life he said he was seeking. For that rich reward is only for those whose hearts are filled to overflowing with love to God and man; love that reveals itself in deeds of mercy and self-sacrifice.

If you and I would have eternal life, our hearts also must be tender with divine compassion for the poor, the sick, the needy, and the oppressed. By deeds of loving-kindness we must prove we are good neighbors, good Samaritans, true children of God.

STORY 4

Lost Sheep and Lost Coins

BECAUSE Jesus talked so much about the love of God and His willingness to forgive the worst of sinners He often had some of the worst characters about town in His audience.

Bad men and bad women came to listen to Him. Bad boys and bad girls too. Thieves, liars, cheats, rogues, ruffians, the very riffraff of society. And they came because He spoke the first word of hope they had ever heard.

Deep in their hearts they wanted to live a better life, but they didn't know how. They thought it wasn't possible. Having fallen into evil ways, they thought they couldn't get out of them. There was no road back—until Jesus came. So they flocked to listen to Him.

To the Pharisees, scribes, lawyers, and other "respectable" people this was all very shocking. "This man receives sinners and eats with them!" they sneered, holding up their hands in horror.

s likened Himself to a faithful shepherd
, although he had ninety-nine sheep safe
e fold, would go out into the mountains to
the one lost sheep that had gone astray.

But this was the finest thing they ever said about Jesus, though they didn't mean it that way. For the chief glory of Jesus is that He does receive sinners. He has been receiving them for a long time now, and still receives them. Even the worst sinners may be sure of a welcome. If you feel you are a sinner, He will receive you right now.

How do I know? Because of what He said to the scribes and Pharisees that day.

"If you had a hundred sheep, and lost one of them, what would you do?" He asked them. "Forget it? No. You would leave the ninety-nine and go after that one lost sheep and search till you found it. Then you would put it on your shoulder and bring it home, calling to your friends and neighbors, 'Rejoice with me, for I have found my sheep which was lost.'"

Every man there knew he would do just that. Some perhaps had already done it, searching patiently for hours, traveling many miles, climbing dangerous mountain trails, risking death past fearful precipices, plodding on through snow and hail and thunderstorm, all for one lost sheep.

For one lost man, one lost boy, one lost girl, however, they wouldn't lift a finger.

But God cares more for the lost man, the lost boy, the lost girl, than for any lost sheep.

"I tell you," said Jesus very earnestly, "there is more joy in heaven over one sinner who repents than over ninety-nine righteous persons who need no repentance."

Then He turned to the women and reminded them of what they do when they lose one little coin.

"Though you have nine coins left in your purse, you will light a lamp and sweep the house and search carefully till you find it. And when you have found it you will call your friends and neighbors and say, 'Rejoice with me, for I have found the coin I lost.' Isn't that so?"

I can see them smiling and nodding their heads. It was exactly so. How well He understood them!

"Likewise," said Jesus, "there is joy among the angels of God over one sinner who repents."

So Jesus became known as the sinners' Friend. He took their part and gave them hope. Even the worst of them, who had wandered the farthest from the fold, now knew that Somebody cared for them and cared enough to come after them and search for them. Most wonderful too was the thought that the angels also cared, and all heaven would ring with joy over every sinner who repented.

Here was love at work again. Love, like a mighty magnet, pulling and tugging at human hearts, breaking the hold of sin and Satan and bringing them home to God.

STORY 5

Lost Boy Found

O F ALL the stories Jesus told, the most touching and beautiful is the one about the runaway boy who came home. It is best known as the story of the Prodigal Son.

"A certain man," said Jesus, "had two sons." Both lived on their father's ranch; both were well off; both were equally loved.

But the younger son was restless. He was tired of being told what to do and what not to do. He wanted to be free to do as he pleased. Most of all, he wanted to enjoy the pleasures of city life he had heard about.

So one day he went to his father and asked for the share of the property that would come to him on his father's death. Of course, he had no right to ask for this now, but his father, loving him dearly, gave it to him.

Soon after, feeling very rich and happy, the boy rode away to the "far country" he had wanted so long to see.

For a while he had a marvelous time. Because of his great riches he made many friends. Between them they spent the money as fast as they could.

Then one day the young man discovered that his money was all gone. He was poor, without a penny left. Now he had no friends; all had left him.

About this time a "mighty famine" struck the "far country." Food ran short. Soon everybody was starving.

Now the young man tried to find work, but the only job he could get was as a swineherd. So hungry did he become that he was tempted to eat the pigs' food.

Then one day as he sat alone with the animals "he came to himself" and thought about all his father's servants and how well they ate all the time. "They have bread enough and to spare, and I perish with hunger!" he said to himself.

Suddenly he made up his mind. "I will arise and go to my father, and will say unto him, Father, I have sinned against heaven, and before thee, and am no more worthy to be called thy son: make me as one of thy hired servants."

117

LOST BOY FOUND

Leaving the pigs, he set off for home. It was a long, long journey, for he had to walk all the way and he was almost worn out with hunger and fatigue.

Every weary mile he wondered what his father would say to him. Perhaps he would refuse even to see him.

But he need not have worried, for every day since he left home his father had been looking for him, hoping he would return.

And now, when his son was still "a great way off," the father saw him, and recognized him, despite his torn clothes, his sagging shoulders, his untidy beard.

Gone were the horses, the fine clothes, and the money-bags with which he had started out, but what did the father care? His boy had come back at last!

With a cry of joy he ran toward him, never stopping till his arms were wrapped around his son.

"Father," he cried, looking up into the tear-stained face above him, "Father, I have sinned against heaven, and in thy sight, and am no more worthy to be called thy son——"

He got no further. By this time several servants had come running up.

"Bring the best robe, and put it on him," ordered the father, now radiantly happy. "And put a ring on his hand and shoes on his feet: and bring hither the fatted calf and kill it; and let us eat, and be merry: for this my son was dead, and is alive again; he was lost, and is found."

Thus did Jesus try to tell the poor sinners how glad God would be if only they, too, would come back to Him.

119

: prodigal son had spent his money and his
lth in wickedness and dissipation, but one
among the swine he realized his sinfulness
resolved to return to his father's house.

But this was not the end of the story. There was the other son to be thought of.

When the older son heard that his brother had been given such a welcome, even though he had behaved so badly and wasted so much money, he was very angry.

"I've served you many years," he said to his father, "and never once broken one of your commandments, but you never gave me even a kid so I could have a feast with my friends. But now this wretched son of yours comes home and, after all he has done, you kill the fatted calf for him!"

"Son," said his father, "you are always with me, and all that is mine is yours. It was fitting that we should make merry and be glad, for this brother of yours was dead, and is alive again; he was lost, and is found."

The brother who stayed at home, who never got into trouble, should have been just as happy about the bad boy's return as was his father. Even so should we rejoice, as God does, over every sinner who comes back to Him.

120

STORY 6

The Wedding Nobody Went To

ONCE upon a time, said Jesus, there was a king who planned a wedding feast for his son. He sent out invitations to all the important people in his kingdom and expected that they would be glad and honored to come.

But they didn't come. One after another sent word to say, "Sorry, but I won't be there."

So the king sent his servants to invite the people personally and urge them to change their minds; but still they would not come.

Some kings would have been very angry at being treated like this; but this one was kind and patient. He decided to give them all one more chance.

As the wedding day drew near he sent out other servants to say to those who had been invited, "Everything is ready; the food is all prepared. Come! Do come!"

But again they refused. In fact, they acted as though they didn't care about the wedding at all. One went off to

121

his farm, another to his place of business. Some even seized the king's servants, beat them up, and killed them.

This was too much for the king. Kind and good though he was, he would not stand for this. So he ordered his soldiers to slay the murderers and burn up their city.

But there were still no guests at the wedding. So now the king called his servants and said to them, "The wedding is ready, but those whom I invited first were not worthy to come. Go now into the streets and invite anyone you meet."

Off they went to do as they were told.

"How would you like to come to the palace tonight?" they asked a beggar on the roadside.

"What, me?" said the poor man, unable to believe his ears.

"Yes, you! Come along. You will be welcome. The king has asked for you. Just make sure you wear a wedding garment."

So they invited everybody they came across, "both bad

and good." Soon hundreds of poor, needy people were hurrying toward the king's palace from all directions.

When all were inside the banquet hall the king came
in to greet them. I can imagine everybody stood and cheered,
so glad were they to be there.

Suddenly, however, there was silence. Something was
wrong. Going up to one of the guests, the king said to him,
"My good man, how did you get in here without a wedding
garment?"

Frightened, the man said nothing. Then, to everybody's
surprise, the king gave orders that he be bound hand and
foot and carried outside.

Such was the story of the royal wedding to which none
of the first invited guests would go.

What was its meaning? Why did Jesus tell it?

The good, kind king, of course, was God, and his son
was Jesus. The invited guests were the leaders of Israel. The
king's servants were the prophets whom God had sent to

them times without number, urging them to repent and return to Him.

What about the people who were found on the streets, the poor and needy, the good and bad? Who were they? They were the men and women, the boys and girls, right in front of Jesus at the time—and everybody like them from that day to this. No doubt it was for them He told the story; to let them know they were welcome, thrice welcome, in His Father's kingdom. They might be the poorest of the poor; they might never have been to school; they might never have had a nice home or a single chance in life; but if they accepted God's loving invitation, they could share the best He had to offer. The wedding feast of the King of heaven was wide open to them.

But there was one condition. Their rags must be covered. They must put on a "wedding garment."

What could that be?

It must be something spotlessly clean, something very, very beautiful. And what else could that be but the purity, the goodness, the forgiving love of Jesus? This glorious garment must be wrapped about all who plan to attend His wedding.

And that means you and me.

STORY 7

The Supper Nobody Wanted

JESUS told another story very much like the one about the royal wedding. Only this one was about a big supper.

"A certain man," He said, "made a great supper and bade many."

At great expense this man had his servants prepare the banquet hall. The long white tables gleamed with sparkling silver and groaned under all the good food piled upon them. Bright lights and soft music made the scene inviting. Only the guests were missing.

They had been invited, but they had not come. They were late. So the man sent his servant to say to them, "Come, for all things are now ready."

But they weren't even interested. Instead, they all began to make excuses.

Said one, "I have bought a piece of ground, and I must go and see it; please excuse me."

Another invited guest said, "I have bought five yoke of

125

oxen and I must go and look them over; please excuse me."

A third said, "I've just got married so I can't come."

They didn't care about the supper. Their minds were on something else. The fact that the good man had gone to so much trouble and expense to make them happy didn't mean a thing to them.

By and by the servant returned to his master and told him what had happened. The good man was very much hurt, as you or I would have been. Then he took one look at the great empty hall with all those long, food-laden tables and said to his servant, "Go out quickly into the streets and lanes of the city, and bring in hither the poor, and the maimed, and the halt, and the blind."

The servant did as he was told, and soon hundreds of eager, happy, hungry beggars were hurrying into the banquet hall.

What a sight that must have been! No lords and ladies there; no rich or famous people; only the common folk from the city streets. Nor did any fancy coronets adorn their heads, or rare jewels sparkle on their fingers; only their faces glowed with the happiness and thankfulness in their hearts.

After a while the flow of people slowed and the servant reported to his master, "There's still room for more."

Happy that so many people had come, the master said, "Go out into the highways and hedges, and compel them to come in, that my house may be filled."

Again the servant obeyed. And this time he really pressed

the people hard. "Come!" he pleaded. "Do come! The supper is ready, and the hall is nearly full."

In this story Jesus revealed again the wonderful love of God for this world. He has gone to great pains to prepare for our happiness. He has made ready a marvelous feast of good things and has invited everybody to share it. But some don't care. They are too busy with plans of their own.

This story of the supper nobody wanted might also be called the story of the Inexcusable Excuses. And we must be careful that we don't use them too.

Maybe you have heard a boy say, "I don't want to go to church today; I've promised the fellows I'd play ball with them."

Or, perhaps you've heard a girl say, "Let's not have worship this evening; there's a program on television we simply mustn't miss."

Or you yourself may have said, "I won't bother to say my prayers tonight; I'm too tired."

These are all excuses for not doing what you know God wants you to do. And they are inexcusable excuses; for there never can be any good excuse for saying, "I don't care what's right"; "I don't care what God says"; or "I don't care whether He's disappointed in me or not."

Such excuses are dangerous. They will lead you to make other excuses later on. And not only could they keep you from the banquet of good things God has prepared for you; they could keep you right out of heaven.

STORY 8

Meanest Man on Earth

JUST to show how mean some people can be, Jesus told this story about a man who had been forgiven a very large debt.

A certain king, He said, decided to check up the accounts of his servants to see whether they had paid all their taxes.

On doing so he discovered that one of them owed him ten thousand talents of silver—an enormous sum of money, such as five million dollars might mean to you or me today.

So he sent for the man and asked him how much he could pay on his debt.

"Nothing," said the man. "I don't have a penny."

He had spent it all.

So the king gave orders that the man, his wife, and his children should be sold as slaves "and payment made."

At this the man fell on his knees and begged the king

for mercy. If only he could have more time, he said, he would pay the debt.

"Have patience with me," he said, "and I will pay you all!"

The king, moved with compassion for the poor man, decided to let him off. So he forgave the entire huge debt and set him free.

How surprised and happy the man must have been! But as he walked out of the gate he ran into a friend of his who owed *him* some money. It wasn't much. Just a few pence. But he made up his mind he would have it now.

"When are you going to pay that debt?" he asked.

"Sorry, but I can't pay it," said his friend, who must have been very poor indeed. "I simply don't have the money."

"Pay me what you owe me!" cried the man, seizing the other by the throat.

"I can't! I can't!" gasped the poor debtor.

"All right, then," snarled the one who had just been forgiven ten thousand talents, "we'll see about that. It's prison for you."

"Have patience with me," cried the other man, "and I will pay you all!"

You would think that the first man would have recognized those words. They were his own plea for mercy to the king. But he didn't. Instead, he hurried his friend off to prison and said he could stay there till he had paid the whole debt.

Fortunately somebody saw what happened and told the king about it. The king couldn't believe that anyone could

8-9

be so mean. So he sent for the man and told him what he thought of him.

"You wicked servant!" he said. "I forgave you all that debt because you asked me. Shouldn't you have had mercy on the one who owed you money, as I had mercy on you?"

Then he gave orders that this meanest of men should be put in prison and kept there till he had paid all the ten thousand talents he had owed.

So the story ended. Now, looking solemnly at the people about Him, Jesus said, "So shall My heavenly Father do to you, if you do not from your hearts forgive your brothers."

It was a great lesson in forgiveness. In His great mercy God is willing to forgive us all our sins; to blot them out and forget them. He is willing to treat us as though we had never done anything wrong. But with like mercy we are to forgive others, *from our hearts.*

The man who was forgiven ten thousand talents and then put his friend in jail because he couldn't pay a hundred pence was surely a mean, cruel man. But was he any meaner than someone today who, having been forgiven all his sins by God, keeps a grudge in his heart toward a fellow man?

How is it with you? Have you forgiven everybody who has hurt you or annoyed you, as God has forgiven you? In any competition to find the meanest person on earth today— the meanest man, the meanest woman, the meanest boy or girl—where would you stand?

STORY 9

Two Boys and Their Dad

ANOTHER story Jesus told was about two boys and a job their father wanted them to do.

One day this father came to one of his sons and said to him, "I want you to work in the vineyard today."

"I won't!" said the boy, and walked off in a huff. He hated working in the vineyard, and anyway there were lots of other things he would rather do.

But as he thought things over he began to feel sorry for the way he had spoken to his father. "Poor old Dad!" he may have said to himself, "I shouldn't have got angry with him. He has an awful lot to do around here. Why didn't I offer to help him?"

Presently the boy decided to go to the vineyard after all, and off he went.

The other son was different. When his father came to him and said, "I want you to work in the vineyard today, son," he answered, "Certainly, Dad. I'll go there right away." But

he never went. In fact, he had no intention of going.

No sooner was his father out of sight than he went fishing, or hunting, or just playing with the neighbor boys. At any rate, he never turned up at the vineyard.

"Which of these two boys," asked Jesus, "obeyed his father? The one who said No and went, or the one who said Yes and didn't go?"

"The first," cried everybody.

"Of course," said Jesus.

Then He pointed out the lesson of His story.

It is much better in God's sight to repent and begin to live right than to make a pretense of doing right and still keep on in one's old, bad ways.

"Some of you," He said, in other words, "went to hear John the Baptist. He preached righteousness and called upon

132

you to repent. Some of you said you would, but you didn't. It was all a pretense. But a lot of poor sinners did repent. They may have been the worst people in the land, but they'll go into heaven before those who just pretend to be good."

Thus once more did Jesus try to get the people to see the importance of true repentance. He wanted them to understand that if they desired to enter heaven and belong to His kingdom of love they must turn from their wicked ways and do the will of God.

It would not be enough for them just to *say* they were going to repent and be good. They would have to *mean* it in their hearts. To say "I repent" and go on living the same old sinful life would be acting a lie—just as the boy did who said he would work in the vineyard and never went near it.

There's a lesson in this story for us too. It's very easy

133

today to make a pretense of being a follower of Jesus. Lots of people claim to be Christians who are not really Christians at all. They say they are on their way to heaven because it sounds nice, but they much prefer to go on enjoying themselves in this old world.

People who act like this will never get to heaven. They just don't belong there. For the kingdom of God is not only a kingdom of love, but a kingdom of honesty, sincerity, purity, goodness, truth.

And if we want to belong to that kingdom, we'll have to fit into God's plans for it. And the only way we can do that is to follow the example of the first boy in the story—the one who repented. He said, "I won't," but on second thought he turned around and said, "I will."

We must do the same.

And it doesn't matter how bad we may have been, or how mean, how rude, how obstinate; if we are willing to change, to repent, to turn rightabout-face, and do God's will, He will receive us with gladness and forgive us all our sins.

Maybe sometime lately you have said, "I won't," to God. "I won't" obey His commandments, or "I won't" go where He asks me, or "I won't" belong to His church, or "I won't" give my heart to Him.

If so, think it over. Remember how dearly He loves you. "Like as a father," the Bible says. Then why not turn to Him at this very moment? Just say, "I'm sorry, Lord; I'm coming after all; I'll do as You say."

He's waiting for you in the vineyard now.

135

d loves every boy and girl who listens to
counsel of his Christian parents, and when
pted to do wrong makes the decision that
matter what comes he will serve the Lord.

STORY 10

Murder in a Vineyard

D ID JESUS actually tell a murder story? He surely did.
There was once a well-to-do householder, He
said, who planted a beautiful vineyard. He thought
so much of it that he couldn't do enough for it.

Carefully he prepared the soil and set out the precious
vines. Then he built a tower for the watchmen and a wine
press to crush the grapes when they should be ripe. Finally
he put a hedge all around to protect it from enemies.

When all this was done he left the place in charge of
workmen he thought he could trust, and went away to another
country.

After a long time the vines became heavy with grapes
and the owner sent his servants to get the fruit.

But when the workmen saw the owner's servants coming
they "beat one, and killed another, and stoned another."

That was the first murder in the vineyard, but not the
last. For when the householder sent another company of

servants to gather the fruit, these also were stoned and killed.

At last the householder said to himself, "I'll send my son. They will surely respect him."

But they didn't. Instead, the workmen said among themselves, "This is the heir; come, let us kill him, and let us seize on his inheritance."

So they murdered the son too.

At this point Jesus asked His listeners what they thought the owner of the vineyard would do to these cruel and unworthy workmen.

They replied, "He will miserably destroy those wicked men, and let out his vineyard to others who will give him its fruit."

Jesus agreed they were right. Then, looking straight at some of the priests and Pharisees who were listening to Him, He said, "The kingdom of God shall be taken from you, and given to a nation bringing forth the fruits thereof."

Now the meaning of this story became plain. Indeed, the Bible says that these priests and Pharisees "perceived" He was talking about them.

The vineyard, of course, was the nation of Israel, planted by God Himself. Tenderly He had cared for it and protected it, expecting a rich harvest of the finest fruit. But when from time to time He had sent His prophets to gather it they had been treated as enemies by the religious leaders who should have welcomed them. Many had been beaten, stoned, and killed. So at last God decided to send His Son. And they

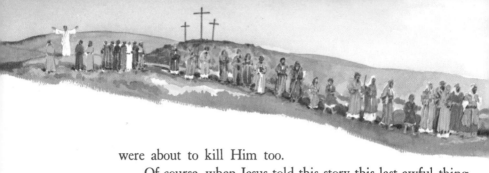

were about to kill Him too.

Of course, when Jesus told this story this last awful thing was still in the future; but the fact that He mentioned it shows that He knew it was going to happen as, a little later, it surely did.

What about the other workmen to whom the vineyard was to be given? These were His disciples—not only the twelve who were with Him then but all who would believe in Him and love Him and work for Him, in years to come. He saw them bringing forth the good fruits of love, truth, and goodness in the lives of countless thousands of others until the final harvest of the vineyard was ripe.

All these dear ones would make up the new nation to whom the kingdom of God would be given. And this nation, not belonging to any one race or people, but gathered from the world out of all "kindreds, and people, and tongues," would

be *His* nation over which He would reign forever and ever.

So would His kingdom come and Eden be restored and the purposes of God be completed.

This story, with all its wonderful meaning, greatly upset the priests and Pharisees who heard it. They saw plainly that

they could have no part in this kingdom Jesus was talking about—not unless they repented; and they had no intention of doing that.

So they became angry with Him, and would have put Him in prison then and there had they dared. But they didn't dare. The Bible says they were afraid of the multitude "because they took Him for a prophet."

All they could do was to go away muttering to each other and planning how they could do the very thing Jesus had told about in His story—murder the Son in His vineyard.

139

STORY 11

Praying and Giving

JESUS was always looking for new stories with great lessons, and more often than not He found them in the lives of people He met and mixed with day by day.

Once while in the Temple He saw two men at prayer, one a Pharisee, the other a publican, or tax collector. The Pharisee was standing where everybody could see and hear him; the other man far in the rear.

In a loud voice the Pharisee was telling God about himself. "God," he cried, "I thank Thee that I am not as other men are, extortioners, unjust, adulterers, or even as this publican. I fast twice in the week, I give tithes of all that I possess."

Then the publican, his hands striking his breast, his head bowed in sorrow of heart, his voice so low it could scarcely be heard, said this brief and humble prayer, "God be merciful to me a sinner."

When Jesus told this story to His disciples some time later, He added, "I tell you, this man [meaning the publican]

141

PAINTING BY HERBERT RUDEEN . © 1956, BY REVIEW AND HERALD

Pharisees liked to appear very pious by
saying long prayers in public places, but
Jesus loved the humble publican more who
prayed "God be merciful to me a sinner."

went down to his house justified rather than the other."

The Pharisee was merely trying to advertise his own good deeds, and God doesn't listen to prayers like that. But when someone whispers, "God be merciful to me a sinner," every word is heard in heaven.

If you want to get through to God sometime, don't tell Him how good you are or how many kind deeds you have done. Just tell Him how much you need His help.

Another time when Jesus was in the Temple He saw something very beautiful happen—something that has been a blessing to millions ever since.

He was sitting quietly near the treasury, watching the people put in their gifts of money. Many rich people came by and gave large sums. Then a poor widow walked slowly up to the box and put in two small coins worth less than a penny.

"Look," Jesus said to His disciples, who were not far

away. "See that poor widow over there? She has just given more than all the rest put together. For they gave out of their abundance, but she in her poverty has given everything she had, all her living."

The widow did not know Jesus was watching her. But He was; and He knew by the look on her face and the prayer on her lips that her gift was from her heart and that it was everything she had.

I like to think that she was rewarded that very day; that angels were sent to supply her needs. But whatever happened to her I know that when Jesus said, "She gave more than all the rest," it was true not only that day, but has been true ever since.

In real value—as God values gifts—her two small coins or "mites" were worth far, far more than all the gold and silver dropped carelessly into the box by the rich people ahead of her.

And when all the money ever given to God is finally added up it may well be found that this poor widow's offering will top the list.

When the widow is shown the total I am sure she will exclaim, "There's been a mistake. I never gave all that!"

But Jesus will say to her, "Oh, but you did. All this was given because of what you gave."

How true! For nineteen hundred years and more the story of this widow's sacrifice has been told and told again. It has gone around the world and echoed down the centuries. More times than anyone could ever count it has touched hearts and opened purses and made people give their best and utmost for the Master.

Of course, it wasn't the amount of the gift that really mattered, but the spirit in which the widow gave it. Her heart must have been God's already before she gave her mites. The two little coins were but final proof that "all that she had" was His.

That is the way we should give to God—from the heart, and with it. Indeed this is the only kind of giving that will be of much help in extending His kingdom of love.

PART IV

Stories of the Prince of Prophets

(MATTHEW 24:1-25:46; MARK 13:1-37; LUKE 17:21-37;
19:12-27; 21:1-36; JOHN 13:36-14:3)

PART FOUR

STORY 1

Homes for the Homeless

JESUS was not only the Prince of healers, the Prince of teachers, and the Prince of storytellers, He was also the Prince of prophets.

He could see into the future. He knew what was going to happen in the days ahead.

Many prophets had spoken to Israel before Jesus came, including Moses, Samuel, Isaiah, Jeremiah, and Daniel. But Jesus was the greatest of them all. He talked about things to come as though He knew all about them.

And there was so much the disciples wanted to know about the future! Like you and me they wanted to see tomorrow as clearly as today.

Once Peter said to Jesus, "We have forsaken all, and followed Thee; what shall we have therefore?"

Jesus had just told His disciples how hard it is for rich people to enter His kingdom; so Peter wanted to know what reward there was for those who had given up everything,

147

PAINTING BY HERBERT RUDEEN   © 1956, BY REVIEW AND HERALD

e of the last lessons Jesus taught His dis-
les was that in heaven there would be no
meless families, for He was going there to
pare mansions for all who loved God.

as he and his friends had done. He was thinking of their boats, their fishing nets, their little homes. They had left everything for Jesus. Now they were poor, with sometimes not even a place to sleep save on the open hillside.

Was it always going to be like this? Would they never have a home again?

For a moment, to cheer them up, Jesus let them look ahead.

"Truly, I say to you," He said, "in the new world, when the Son of man shall sit on His glorious throne, you who have followed Me will also sit on twelve thrones, judging the twelve tribes of Israel. And every one who has left houses or brothers or sisters or father or mother or children or lands, for My name's sake, will receive a hundredfold, and inherit eternal life."

I can see Peter, James, John, and the rest of them smiling at each other as Jesus made this promise. To think that they, just humble folk from Galilee, would be the chief judges of Israel! How wonderful! Yes! And at last they would all have nice houses to live in. Never again would they have to wander from place to place, hungry, thirsty, and homeless.

148

But there was something else they wanted to know. For some time now Jesus had been dropping hints that He wouldn't be with them much longer.

"Little children," He said to them once, very tenderly, "I shall only be with you a little while now, and where I am going you cannot come."

Peter was worried. An awful lonesomeness clutched at his heart.

"Lord, where are You going?" he asked.

"Where I am going you can't follow Me now," said Jesus. "But you shall follow Me afterward."

"Why can't I follow You now?" asked Peter.

He was puzzled. So were the rest of the disciples. They could not bring themselves to believe that in "a little while" their beloved Master would leave them. And if He did, what would happen to all His promises of houses and friends and loved ones and life everlasting?

Perhaps, they thought, He was planning to go to Greece or Italy and would soon be back again. Some of the Jews even asked, "Does He intend to go . . . and teach the Greeks?" (John 7:35, R.S.V.).

But Jesus didn't mean that. He was going much farther away than Athens or Rome. He was going back to heaven, whence He had come to this earth.

"Let not your heart be troubled," He said to them in words that will live forever. "Ye believe in God, believe also in Me. In My Father's house are many mansions: if it were not so, I would have told you. I go to prepare a place for you. And if I go and prepare a place for you, I will come again, and receive you unto Myself; that where I am, there ye may be also."

He could not have spoken more plainly. He was going far away—to His Father's house.

Maybe He was looking up at the stars as He spoke. Somewhere at the heart and hub of this great shining universe He would meet the One who had sent Him, and whom He so dearly loved.

But no matter how far He went, or how long He stayed away, He would never forget His disciples. No, indeed. Instead He would prepare a place for them and make it lovelier each passing day.

There would be lots of room for all of them. Among the thousand billion orbs He had created there were "many mansions," or "abiding places"—enough for all who loved Him. There would be a mansion for Peter, another for James, and another for John. And there would be one each for all of His faithful followers. None would be homeless any more.

STORY 2

Space Flight Promised

H OW WOULD the disciples ever get the lovely homes Jesus promised them?

"I will come again," He assured them, "and receive you unto Myself; that where I am, there ye may be also."

This was a solemn promise, and we may be certain He will keep it. True, He has not come back yet; He is still in His Father's house; but someday He will return for His own.

And that means space flight for all of His faithful followers.

It's marvelous to think about; but nineteen hundred years ago, long before all the modern talk about voyages to the moon, long before little boys were buying space helmets and little girls were dreaming of trips to Mars and Venus, Jesus told His disciples they would someday journey through the universe. When He comes back to this earth again He will "receive" His people to Himself and lead them out through "the wild blue yonder" to His Father's house.

Nor will it be only Peter, James, and John who will enjoy this rare privilege. All who have loved Jesus and been loyal to Him will be able to go along too.

The apostle Paul was very clear about this. When he wrote to the Christians at Thessalonica, he said, "The Lord Himself shall descend from heaven with a shout, with the voice of the archangel, and with the trump of God: and the dead in Christ shall rise first: then we which are alive and remain shall be caught up together with them in the clouds, to meet the Lord in the air: and so shall we ever be with the Lord."

Imagine it! "Caught up together . . . in the clouds, to meet the Lord in the air!" How very, very thrilling! Sailing out toward the moon! Flying from planet to planet! Off to the stars! It seems impossible, but it must be true, for Jesus has promised it.

HERBERT RUDEEN, ARTIST

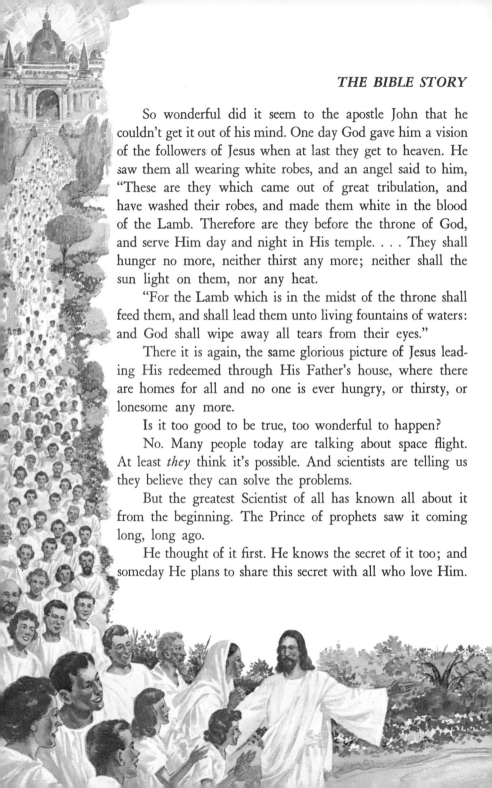

So wonderful did it seem to the apostle John that he couldn't get it out of his mind. One day God gave him a vision of the followers of Jesus when at last they get to heaven. He saw them all wearing white robes, and an angel said to him, "These are they which came out of great tribulation, and have washed their robes, and made them white in the blood of the Lamb. Therefore are they before the throne of God, and serve Him day and night in His temple. . . . They shall hunger no more, neither thirst any more; neither shall the sun light on them, nor any heat.

"For the Lamb which is in the midst of the throne shall feed them, and shall lead them unto living fountains of waters: and God shall wipe away all tears from their eyes."

There it is again, the same glorious picture of Jesus leading His redeemed through His Father's house, where there are homes for all and no one is ever hungry, or thirsty, or lonesome any more.

Is it too good to be true, too wonderful to happen?

No. Many people today are talking about space flight. At least *they* think it's possible. And scientists are telling us they believe they can solve the problems.

But the greatest Scientist of all has known all about it from the beginning. The Prince of prophets saw it coming long, long ago.

He thought of it first. He knows the secret of it too; and someday He plans to share this secret with all who love Him.

STORY 3

Jesus Unveils the Future

A S THE disciples talked among themselves about the wonderful things Jesus had told them they longed to know more about the future.

If He was going to leave them, what would happen to them after He was gone? How long would He be away? When would this present world end and *His* world, His beautiful kingdom of love, begin?

At last they found a chance to ask Him.

One day, while looking at the massive walls of the Temple, Jesus startled them all by saying, "You see all these things? There shall not be left one stone upon another that will not be thrown down."

The disciples could hardly believe their ears. The Temple destroyed! How could that ever happen? Such a beautiful building too, and so costly! Who would ever want to wreck it? Perhaps Jesus meant He was going to throw it down Himself when He came to set up His kingdom. Or would it be the work of enemies? They made up their minds to find out.

Back on the Mount of Olives, where the little group often met, they asked Him.

"Tell us," they said, "when shall these things be? and what shall be the sign of Thy coming, and of the end of the world?"

Jesus told them. Drawing back the curtain that hides the future, He let them look into the years ahead.

It was not a bit as they had expected. Indeed, I wouldn't be surprised if afterward they wished they hadn't asked Him. Sometimes it's better not to know the future, but to leave it in the hands of God.

First, Jesus warned them to be ever on the watch for false christs. He said that after He had gone away one man after another would arise and say, "I am Christ," and claim to have come back just as Jesus promised He would do.

As for the promised kingdom, that would not be set up for a long time yet.

"You shall hear of wars and rumours of wars," He said.

"For nation shall rise against nation, and kingdom against kingdom: and there shall be famines, and pestilences, and earthquakes, in divers places."

All these terrible things would be but "the beginning of sorrows." Far worse troubles would come to the disciples. They would be cruelly treated. Enemies would put them in prison and kill them.

"You shall be hated of all nations for My name's sake," said Jesus.

Because of all this suffering many who claimed to be His followers would give up their faith "and betray one another, and . . . hate one another." Wickedness would abound and love grow cold.

Some faithful ones, however, would never give up. They would endure to the end and be saved.

Jesus now began to talk about Jerusalem, which at this moment lay peacefully below them. Great trouble would come upon this city, He said, and soon. A foreign army would utterly destroy it.

The disciples could save themselves from this disaster by watching for a certain sign. The moment they saw the city surrounded by soldiers they were to flee to a place of safety. They must not delay a moment, not even to pick up a single treasure. Should they be working in a field they must not go home to get their clothes. Instead, they must run for dear life. Should they do so, they would have just enough time to escape.

Then Jesus said a strange thing. He told them to pray that they wouldn't have to flee in the winter or on the Sabbath day.

On that quiet, peaceful afternoon on the Mount of Olives it must have been hard for the disciples to imagine the scenes Jesus was talking about. Their lives in dear old Galilee had been so peaceful. They had never seen a great city besieged by armies. And the very idea of their holy city being destroyed was frightening to them. Would it really happen?

Later they told other disciples what Jesus had said, and the news spread far and wide.

JESUS UNVEILS THE FUTURE

Many believers began to pray that their flight might not be on the Sabbath or in the winter. No doubt some wondered how they would be able to flee if Jerusalem were surrounded by an army. It did seem strange, come to think of it. But they went on believing that Jesus couldn't have made a mistake.

Of course, He hadn't. About forty years later Jerusalem was surrounded by Roman soldiers. Recognizing the promised sign, the Christians in the city prepared to flee. Then, just as they were wondering how they would get through the enemy lines, the Romans mysteriously withdrew. Every follower of Jesus who believed His warning got away. Then the Romans returned and destroyed the city.

How wonderful that Jesus should have known all this so long before it happened! But there, was He not the Prince of prophets?

Back on that lonely hillside He now began to tell His disciples about other things that would happen hundreds of years ahead—right on down to the end of time.

STORY 4

Signs of His Coming

LOOKING far into the future, Jesus told His disciples about a fearful time of trouble that would come upon all who loved Him.

"Then shall be great tribulation," He said, "such as was not since the beginning of the world to this time, no, nor ever shall be."

No doubt He was thinking of the days of trouble the prophet Daniel wrote about. Perhaps you remember that "little horn" on the head of the fourth beast, which wore out "the saints of the most High." Jesus knew this story well. He was the One who had sent Gabriel to tell Daniel about it. Now, as He retold it to His disciples, He was sad for His "elect"— His dear people who would suffer so much.

As the days of sorrow and suffering would slowly pass, more and more cheats would claim to be Christ, come back from heaven. So weary would the people be, so eager for the trouble to end, that many would be deceived.

160

False christs and false prophets would arise, showing "great signs and wonders." But, said Jesus, don't follow them.

If anyone says to you, Lo, here is Christ, or, There He is! don't believe it.

If they say, Behold He is in the desert, don't go to look for Him there.

If they say, Behold He is in some secret room, don't believe it. He won't be there either.

They were to watch for certain great happenings, each one so big and important that no deceiver could imitate it. The first would be in the heavens, which God would use as a huge advertising sign.

"There shall be signs in the sun, and in the moon, and in the stars," said Jesus. "The sun shall be darkened, and the moon shall not give her light, and the stars shall fall from heaven."

8-11

The next signs would be on the earth. "Upon the earth distress of nations, with perplexity; the sea and the waves roaring; men's hearts failing them for fear, and for looking after those things which are coming on the earth: for the powers of heaven shall be shaken."

Right after this, said Jesus, everybody will "see the Son of man coming in a cloud with power and great glory."

Believers in Jesus should watch very carefully for these signs because they are the sure tokens of His Second Advent.

"When these things begin to come to pass," He said, "then look up, and lift up your heads; for your redemption draweth nigh."

Pointing to a fig tree not far away, He reminded His disciples how the bursting forth of nature in the springtime is looked upon by all as a sure sign of the coming of summer.

"So," He said, "when you see all these things come to pass, know . . . that the kingdom of God is nigh at hand."

The promised signs in the heavens and on the earth—great, marvelous, and unmistakable—will herald His glorious return.

At this point, of course, you are probably asking, Have these things happened? Have people seen them?

That's worth thinking about; for nobody would want to be taken by surprise. How sad it would be to have Jesus come back some day and no one be ready to welcome Him!

Many people believe that most of these signs have already appeared, for near the end of the long period of trial for the true church of Jesus, foretold by Daniel, several mysterious and wonderful sights caused many people to think the coming of Jesus was near.

The first of these was the famous Dark Day of New England, May 19, 1780, when the sun became dark at midday. That night the moon also was darkened.

Then some years later, the world witnessed the greatest shower of meteors in history, known as the falling of the stars of November 12-13, 1833. The people who saw the wonderful sight took it for the sign Jesus promised.

As for the signs upon the earth—the "distress of nations, with perplexity," with men's hearts "failing them for fear" as they look at the things "which are coming on the earth"— can they not all be seen now? Daddy and Mother can tell you about the dreadful world wars they remember. And the practice air raid warnings you hear every now and then let you know how afraid everybody is of the atomic bomb and the hydrogen bomb and all the other fearful weapons recently invented. Yes, and the jet planes whining and roaring overhead tell us that the worst things we've ever feared could happen so quickly we'd scarcely have time to think what to do.

Perhaps it was because Jesus knew all about these things and, as the Prince of prophets, could see them far on down the years, that He urged His disciples to be careful lest they become so careless, or so busy, that they would fail to see the signs, big and plain though they might be. He didn't want that day of days to come upon them "as a snare," with the suddenness that a trap closes upon an unwary animal.

"Watch at all times," He said to them and to us, "praying that you may have strength to escape all these things that will take place, and to stand before the Son of man."

STORY 5

More Signs for All to See

AS JESUS warned His disciples to watch for His return I can imagine they said to Him, "Don't worry, Lord; we won't forget; we'll be looking for You; we'll be glad to see You again."

But Jesus knew better. He knew that, after many years had passed, even those who claimed to love Him most would begin to wonder whether He would ever come back. Some would say, "My Lord delayeth His coming" and give up the faith altogether.

Once He said that His return will be very much like the coming of the great Flood in the days of Noah.

"As it was in the days of Noah," He said, "so will it be in the days of the Son of man. They ate, they drank, they married, they were given in marriage, *until the day* when Noah entered the ark, and the flood came and destroyed them all. . . . So will it be on the day when the Son of man is revealed."

165

Everyday things will go on much the same right on down to the end. Mothers will get breakfast, wash the dishes, make the beds, clean the house, and so on, just as they have always done. Fathers will shave and eat and rush off to work as usual. Boys and girls will get out of bed, throw on their clothes, eat their breakfast, and run to school just as they do all the time. In other words, most people will be acting just about as usual "until the day" that Jesus appears in His glory. That's why we must be so very careful to be ready for His coming all the time.

Just because life seems to go along much the same from day to day we must never let ourselves say, "Oh, well, nothing's going to happen; the world is going to go on and on as it is forever." If we do, we shall be taken by surprise. For Jesus will break in upon us suddenly, when we least expect Him, as "a thief in the night," or as the fire fell upon Sodom and Gomorrah, or as the Flood came upon the world of Noah.

Maybe we should look a little more closely at those words of Jesus: "As it was in the days of Noah, so will it be in the days of the Son of man."

How were things back then? What were the days of Noah like?

If you want to know, just turn back to the first few chapters of the book of Genesis.

Did you ever notice that after Cain killed Abel, and fled eastward from Eden to the land of Nod, his son Enoch built a city? That was the first city ever built. It may have been a small one, but it marked the beginning of a trend

away from country living to city living with all its evils.

Did you ever notice that Cain's great-great-grandson Lamech was the first man to take two wives? That's when polygamy began, with all its sad results.

One of Lamech's sons, Jubal, was a great musician—"the father of all such as handle the harp and organ." What sort of tunes he taught the people to play we are not told, but no doubt he filled the days of Noah with music of one kind or another.

His brother Tubal-cain was skilled in the production of "brass and iron." He started the steel industry. We should not think of these men of long ago as ignorant cave men. They were closely related to Adam, who was still alive. They had keen minds and skilled hands. They must have invented all sorts of useful things, such as tools for their trades and furniture for their homes.

But with all their skill these men could not keep themselves from evil. Of Lamech it is said that he boasted having killed a man who struck him. This murder led to others until "the earth was filled with violence."

Things got so bad that "God saw that the wickedness of man was great in the earth, and that every imagination of the thoughts of his heart was only evil continually. And it repented the Lord that He had made man on the earth, and it grieved Him at His heart. And the Lord said, I will destroy man whom I have created from the face of the earth."

No doubt Jesus had all this in His mind when He said, "As it was in the days of Noah, so will it be in the days of the Son of man."

We have the city builders today, don't we? How many they have built, all around the world, each one a stronghold of sin!

We have the makers of music, too, and what horrible music much of it is! Jubal-cain would be ashamed of it.

We have also the mighty men of industry, with their vast iron and steel works and their factories for producing metals and machinery and weapons of every kind.

What of the family troubles of the days of Noah? Do we have those too?

Do we! Lamech took two wives, which was bad enough; but nowadays some men take four or five, one after another. People divorce and remarry over and over again. Families are carelessly broken up and children left motherless and fatherless. Surely Noah saw nothing quite so bad as this in the days before the Flood.

As for violence, which "filled the earth" in those far-off days, there is more of it now than then. And nowadays it is taught in the home. Think of all the killing that goes on in the stories presented on television. All day long somebody is being shot or stabbed or poisoned.

I hope you don't look at programs that show how horrid and wicked people can be. Why? Because little by little such pictured sin will make you think that evil isn't really evil; that there's nothing wrong about being cruel, deceitful, or dishonorable, if you can get away with it. Such ideas, if you become familiar with them, will lead you clear away from what is right and true and beautiful. They will cause you to hate God and His commandments. Evil will become attractive and you will begin to imagine that you can do anything you please without fear of punishment.

Lots of boys and girls have reached that place now. Pretty soon, as Jesus has warned us, we shall see conditions as they were in the days of Noah when "every imagination of the thoughts" of people's hearts "was only evil continually."

So if you want to see more signs of the coming of Jesus, all you have to do is to look about you. They are everywhere. Some of them are right in your own home.

STORY 6

How Jesus Will Return

TO MAKE sure that His disciples should not be misled by some false teacher, Jesus told them exactly how He would return.

He will not come secretly, He said, but openly so that the whole world may see Him. He will be as visible as lightning.

"As the lightning comes from the east and shines as far as the west, so will be the coming of the Son of man."

Fog can hide a searchlight, or the landing lights on an airfield, but nothing can hide the lightning. The darkest clouds only help to make it seem more brilliant. So will Christ's coming be glorious beyond words and seen by everyone.

"All the tribes of the earth," He said, "shall see the Son of man coming in the clouds of heaven with power and great glory." That means everybody in Europe, Asia, Africa, America, and Australia. It takes in the white race, the black race, the yellow race, and all the rest. It includes Americans, English-

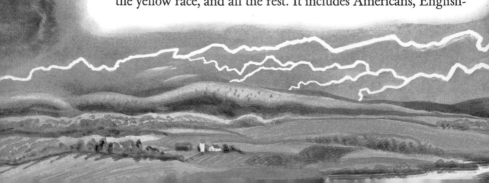

men, Frenchmen, Germans, Swiss, Russians, South Africans, New Zealanders, Chinese, Indians, Hottentots, and everybody else. All the tribes, all the nations, all the people, without exception, will see Him come.

And He will not come silently. There will be lots of noise, so that even the deaf will know He is on His royal way. For He "shall send His angels with a great sound of a trumpet, and they shall gather together His elect from the four winds, from one end of heaven to the other."

It must have been these words of the Master that the apostle Paul had in mind when he said that the Lord will "descend from heaven with a shout, with the voice of the archangel, and with the trump of God."

John remembered them too when he wrote, "And the heaven departed as a scroll when it is rolled together; and every mountain and island were moved out of their places. And the kings of the earth, and the great men, and the rich men, and the chief captains, and the mighty men, . . . hid themselves in the dens and in the rocks of the mountains; and said to the mountains and rocks, Fall on us, and hide us from the face

of Him that sitteth on the throne, and from the wrath of the Lamb: for the great day of His wrath is come; and who shall be able to stand?"

So Jesus, the Prince of prophets, left no doubt as to how He will return. When He descends the skies everybody will see Him and everybody will hear Him. And there won't be any doubt as to who is coming. Everyone will know it is Jesus of Nazareth, the Messiah of Israel, the Son of God, now crowned King of kings and Lord of lords.

There's one important thing we do not know about His Second Advent, and that is exactly when He will come. The fulfillment of the promised signs tells us He is near, but the actual day is a secret known only to God.

Jesus made this very, very plain. "Of that day and hour knoweth no man, no, not the angels of heaven, but My Father only."

After all, it's better that way. If we knew the very day of His coming, we might put off getting ready to meet Him till the night before. Many people would do just that. And they would postpone repentance till too late.

Not knowing the day, we must be ready all the time. And that's exactly what Jesus asks of us.

"Watch therefore," He says, "for you do not know on what day your Lord is coming. . . . Therefore you also must be ready; for the Son of man is coming at an hour you do not expect."

He's going to surprise us all. May it be a happy surprise for you and me.

173

has promised that when He comes the
d time everybody will see Him. Although
gns of His coming are on every hand, no
nows the day or hour of His appearing.

STORY 7

Radio and Television Foreseen

A S JESUS talked with His disciples about His return He gave them one other sign that could be the most important of all.

"This gospel of the kingdom," He said, "shall be preached in all the world for a witness unto all nations; and then shall the end come."

"This gospel of the kingdom" is, of course, the good news about His plans for the future of this world and the people who live on it. It includes the story of His coming from heaven to live among men; the story of His suffering and death; the story of His resurrection and ascension; and the story of His coming again in glory to set up His kingdom of love and restore all that was lost in Eden.

When this beautiful gospel has been preached in all the world, and everybody in all the nations has had a chance to hear it, "then shall the end come."

Jesus did not say that all the people who hear the gospel

will become Christians. No. What He said was that this gospel would be preached "as a witness" unto all nations. People everywhere would hear it, and make up their minds whether they wanted to belong to His kingdom of love.

When you stop to think of it, this was a very wonderful prophecy Jesus made. In those days there was but one great empire in all the world, and that was Rome. Nobody had ever heard of the United States, or France, or Germany, or Russia. England was not even yet invaded by the Roman army. China, India, and Africa were lands of mystery to most of the people of Palestine.

Yet the Prince of prophets dared to say that the glorious news about His kingdom would be carried to the ends of the earth and to nations yet unborn.

Looking down the centuries, He saw them all, with all their languages, customs, and many-colored flags.

"All these," He said, "shall hear My gospel—and then shall the end come."

He must have known that this would mean translating

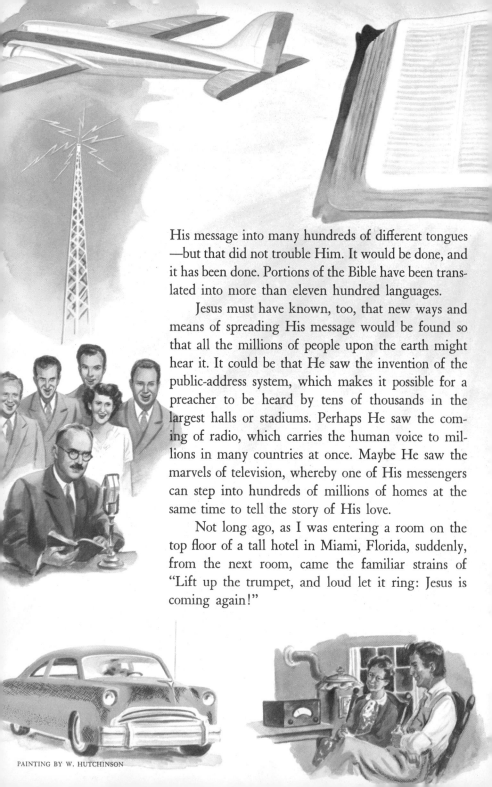

His message into many hundreds of different tongues —but that did not trouble Him. It would be done, and it has been done. Portions of the Bible have been translated into more than eleven hundred languages.

Jesus must have known, too, that new ways and means of spreading His message would be found so that all the millions of people upon the earth might hear it. It could be that He saw the invention of the public-address system, which makes it possible for a preacher to be heard by tens of thousands in the largest halls or stadiums. Perhaps He saw the coming of radio, which carries the human voice to millions in many countries at once. Maybe He saw the marvels of television, whereby one of His messengers can step into hundreds of millions of homes at the same time to tell the story of His love.

Not long ago, as I was entering a room on the top floor of a tall hotel in Miami, Florida, suddenly, from the next room, came the familiar strains of "Lift up the trumpet, and loud let it ring: Jesus is coming again!"

PAINTING BY W. HUTCHINSON

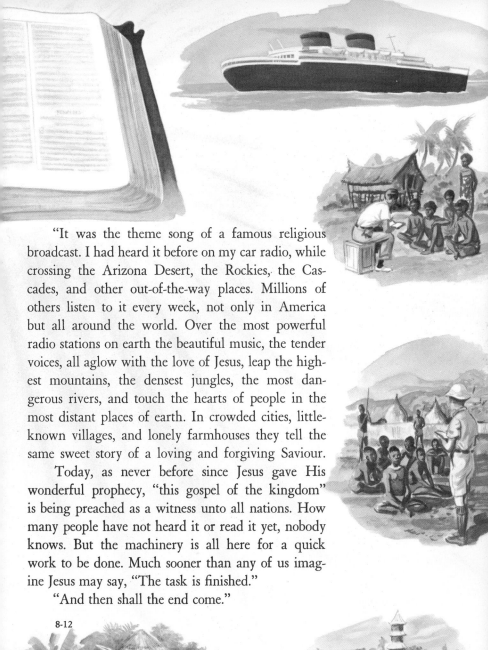

"It was the theme song of a famous religious broadcast. I had heard it before on my car radio, while crossing the Arizona Desert, the Rockies, the Cascades, and other out-of-the-way places. Millions of others listen to it every week, not only in America but all around the world. Over the most powerful radio stations on earth the beautiful music, the tender voices, all aglow with the love of Jesus, leap the highest mountains, the densest jungles, the most dangerous rivers, and touch the hearts of people in the most distant places of earth. In crowded cities, little-known villages, and lonely farmhouses they tell the same sweet story of a loving and forgiving Saviour.

Today, as never before since Jesus gave His wonderful prophecy, "this gospel of the kingdom" is being preached as a witness unto all nations. How many people have not heard it or read it yet, nobody knows. But the machinery is all here for a quick work to be done. Much sooner than any of us imagine Jesus may say, "The task is finished."

"And then shall the end come."

8-12

STORY 8

Ten Sleepy Girls

ONE OF the most exciting stories Jesus told was about ten sleepy girls. They were bridesmaids, all dressed up for a wedding, all eager to take part in it, and half of them never got there!

As the ceremony was to be held in the evening, each girl had a little oil lamp to carry. I am sure all of them looked forward eagerly to taking part in the procession. Just in case anything should go wrong, five of them had brought along a little extra oil.

Since it was an Eastern wedding, they were all waiting at the bride's house—not for the bride, but for the bridegroom. It was the custom for him to come to the home of the bride and lead her away to his own.

The girls weren't sleepy at first, of course. I suppose they were as happy and gay as most bridesmaids usually are, as they talked about the bride, the bridegroom, and their own chances of getting married. But as time went on and the bridegroom did not appear they began to yawn and grow drowsy. No longer did they stand on tiptoe looking for the procession to come. Instead they sat down on the grass and grumbled at the delay.

"Whatever can have happened?" sighed one. "I wish the bridegroom would hurry up."

"I'm going to have five minutes' sleep," said another. "I'm tired; wake me up, girls, when you see him coming."

At this she lay down and was soon fast asleep. Another girl followed suit. Then another and another until "they all slumbered and slept."

One by one the little lamps flickered and went out. By and by the only light came from the stars shining overhead.

Hour after hour went by, and the ten sleepy girls slept on.

Suddenly, at midnight, they heard somebody shouting,

"The bridegroom's coming! Everybody go to meet him!"

The girls stirred and awoke. They rubbed their eyes. The procession was indeed coming down the street. They jumped to their feet, straightening their dresses and patting their hair in place. Then they remembered their lamps. All were out, and the wicks were thick with carbon. Quickly the girls began to trim them, for they couldn't join the procession without their lamps.

Then five of them made a terrible discovery. They had no oil.

"Lend us some of yours!" they begged the others.

"Sorry," said the others; "but we don't have a drop to spare."

"But what shall we do? We'll miss the wedding!" cried the five who had no oil.

"Better go and buy some," said the others.

"What? At this time of night?"

"There might be a store open. You could try."

Frantically the five dashed off into the darkness.

While they were gone "the bridegroom came; and they that were ready went in with him to the marriage: and the door was shut."

Then the saddest thing happened. The five girls who had gone off looking for oil came back, breathless with running. But they were too late. They had missed both the procession and the wedding.

They banged on the door, crying, "Let us in, let us in!" But nobody opened it. The bridegroom merely called from within, "I don't know you."

The lesson here is that we must always be ready for His return. "Watch therefore," He said, "for you know neither the day nor the hour when the Son of man comes."

It could well be that, as the Prince of prophets, He was looking down the long, long years to our time. Perhaps He was thinking of you and me, knowing how easy it is for us to give up hope in His coming and get careless and sleepy and let our lamps go out.

"Watch!" He says to us. "Keep awake! Look out for the signs of My return!"

Someday the cry will be heard again, "Behold, the bridegroom cometh!" From city to city, from country to country, the wonderful news will spread like wildfire, "Jesus is coming!"

Some will be ready to meet Him; some will not.

Some will go to heaven with Him, and some will be left out.

In which group will you be?

Let us all be ready with our lamps trimmed and burning till He comes.

STORY 9

Tale of the Talents

KNOWING that He would soon be leaving His disciples and going away for a long, long time, Jesus tried to give them all the good advice He could so that they would know what to do while He was gone.

That is why He told them the story of the ten sleepy girls. He wanted them to be ready always for His return. But just being ready was not enough. They must make the most of their lives, serving God faithfully every day and using every chance to tell others of His love.

To make this plain, Jesus told another story. This was about a merchant who went on a long trip into a far country. Before leaving, this man called three of his servants and handed each of them a certain amount of money—"to every man according to his several ability" to use it.

To one he gave five talents, to another two talents, and to the third, one talent. Then, after urging each to do his best, he went on his journey.

The man with the five talents started to work at once, buying and selling until he had made his five talents ten.

The man with the two talents did the same, only he didn't earn quite so much. Even so he made a one-hundred-percent gain, so that his two talents became four.

But the man with the one talent merely dug a hole in the ground, buried his talent, and took life easy. He told his friends that he didn't see why he should work while the boss was away on a vacation.

By and by the merchant returned and called his servants to account for the money he had entrusted to them.

The first came and told how he had traded with the five talents and earned five more.

"Well done, good and faithful servant!" said his master. "You have been faithful over a little, I will set you over much."

Then the second servant told what he had done.

"Master," he said, "you gave me two talents; here are two more."

"Well done, good and faithful servant!" said the master. "You have been faithful over a little; I will set you over much."

Lastly the one-talent man came to report. He was a surly sort of fellow. "Master," he said, "I knew you were the kind of man who just makes profit out of other men's work, so I buried your old talent. Here it is. Take it. You can have it back."

At this the merchant was very upset. "You wicked and lazy servant!" he said. "Why didn't you at least put my money in the bank so I could have gained interest on it?"

Then he added, "Take the talent from him and give it to the man with the ten talents. And throw this worthless servant outside in the dark."

There is a lesson here for all of us. The merchant in this story is Jesus. He has gone away to a far country. And to each of His disciples He has given talents, according to his ability. Some have five talents, some two, some only one. But He expects all to use them the best they know how.

Someday, when He returns, He is going to ask us what we have done with all the good gifts He has given us.

Oh, but you say, He never gave *me* any money.

Maybe not. But money isn't the only talent. Your voice is a talent, with the power to talk and sing. Your brain is a talent, with the power to think and plan. Your hands are a talent, with the power to write, to play music, to do good to the needy.

Stop a moment right now and count your talents. You will probably find that you have more than five, maybe ten. And Jesus wants you to use them all to His glory.

Perhaps you are saying, "But I've only got one talent." All right. Just don't bury it. Make the most of it. Use it, and watch it grow!

It's not the number of talents we have that matters, but how faithful we are in using them. Jesus wants us to be "faithful in that which is least"—in the few things, the littlest things, we do for Him.

And when the day of reckoning comes, how happy you will be to hear Jesus say to you, "Well done, good and faithful servant!"

That "Well done!" said with a smile and a handshake, will be reward enough for anything any of us ever did for Him.

STORY 10

Passport to Heaven

A FTER telling His disciples to be ever on the watch for His return and, in the meantime, to make the most of all the talents He had given them, Jesus drew back the curtain of the future once more and let them glimpse the wonderful scene when He will sit at last upon His throne of glory as King of kings and Lord of lords.

"When the Son of man comes in His glory," He said, "and all the angels with Him, then He will sit on His glorious throne. Before Him will be gathered all the nations, and He will separate them one from another, as a shepherd separates the sheep from the goats: and He will place the sheep at His right hand, but the goats at the left."

As the disciples pictured this happy day, their eyes sparkled with gladness. How they wanted their Master to be a king! How they longed to see His dream of a worldwide kingdom of love come true! How they hoped that they might have a part in it some day!

But what was this about sheep and goats? Who were the sheep and who were the goats? And how would Jesus separate them?

Eagerly they waited for the rest of the story. And Jesus said, "Then the King will say to those at his right hand, 'Come, O blessed of My Father, inherit the kingdom prepared for you from the foundation of the world: for I was hungry and you gave Me food, I was thirsty and you gave Me drink, I was a stranger and you welcomed Me, I was naked and you clothed Me, I was sick and you visited Me, I was in prison and you came to Me.'

"Then the righteous will answer Him, 'Lord, when did we see Thee hungry and feed Thee, or thirsty and give Thee drink? And when did we see Thee a stranger and welcome Thee, or naked and clothe Thee? And when did we see Thee sick or in prison and visit Thee?'

"And the King will answer them, Truly, I say unto you, as you did it to one of the least of these My brethren, you did it to Me."

These are the sheep. Christ's sheep. They stand at His right hand. They are the men and women, the boys and girls, who show kindness to others, whose hearts are filled with love and sympathy for the least of His brethren. They inherit His kingdom.

And the goats? They are the little, selfish people who never give a thought to other people's needs and sufferings.

To them Jesus will say, "I was hungry, and you gave Me no food, I was thirsty, and you gave Me no drink. I was

en the King will say to those at His right
d, 'Come, O blessed of My Father, inherit
kingdom prepared for you.'" And with
the faithful will enter the city of God.

a stranger, and you did not welcome Me, naked, and you did not clothe Me, sick and in prison, and you did not visit Me."

They will answer, "Lord, when did we see Thee hungry or thirsty or a stranger or naked or sick or in prison, and did not minister to Thee?"

And He will answer them, "Truly, I say to you, as you did it not to one of the least of these, you did it not for Me."

For these there will be no kingdom, no heaven, no eternal happiness. Instead they will share the punishment of the devil and his angels. Jesus said so Himself.

So it is love that makes the difference. It is love that separates those who are saved from those who are lost. It is love that decides whether we shall be among the sheep or the goats in the day of judgment.

Love is the passport to heaven. If we do not have it in our hearts—if we do not show it by gracious words and kindly

deeds, we shall never enter the kingdom of God. For His kingdom is a kingdom of love. It is made up of a people who love one another. And its King is the King of love.

And if love is so very important, maybe we should be looking around to see whether there is anyone who needs to be loved by us.

Think a moment. Is there somebody you know who is hungry, somebody whom you could feed? Maybe some poor little boy at school would be glad for a part of your lunch some day. Or a drink out of your nice new vacuum bottle.

And what about that new girl in your class, or the one who has just come to live next door? Are you being as friendly as you should? Have you said, "Welcome!" and meant it?

Maybe there's somebody you know who doesn't have money enough to buy clothes to keep himself warm. Could you share some of yours?

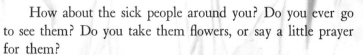

How about the sick people around you? Do you ever go to see them? Do you take them flowers, or say a little prayer for them?

Do you have a friend in prison? Do you ever go to see him or write him a note of sympathy?

Remember that whatever you do like this out of a love-filled heart is reckoned by Jesus to have been done for Him. And He will never forget the kindness. Not through all eternity.

Every time He meets you in His kingdom He will say, "Thank you for being so kind to Me." And you will say, "Lord, when was I kind to You?" And He will smile and say, "When you shared your lunch with Tommy, when you cried with Susan, and when you visited your lonely old grandma."

And you will say, "But Jesus, I didn't think that was helping You!"

"But it was," He will say. "Inasmuch as you loved one of the least of these My children, you were loving Me."

How glad we all shall be for every deed of love we ever did!